F-4 PHANTOM II
VS
MiG-21

USAF & VPAF in the Vietnam War

PETER DAVIES

First published in Great Britain in 2008 by Osprey Publishing,
Midland House, West Way, Botley, Oxford OX2 0PH, UK
443 Park Avenue South, New York, NY 10016, USA

E-mail: info@ospreypublishing.com

A CIP catalogue record for this book is available from the British Library

ISBN: 978 1 84603 316 2

Edited by Tony Holmes
Cockpit artwork by Jim Laurier
Cover artwork, battlescene and gunsight view by Gareth Hector
Three-views and armament scrap views by Tom Tullis
Page layouts by Myriam Bell Design, France
Index by Alan Thatcher
Typeset in Adobe Garamond and ITC Conduit
Maps by Bounford.com, Huntingdon, UK
Originated by PDQ Digital Media Solutions
Printed in China through Bookbuilders

08 09 10 11 12   10 9 8 7 6 5 4 3 2 1

FOR A CATALOGUE OF ALL BOOKS PUBLISHED BY OSPREY MILITARY
AND AVIATION PLEASE CONTACT:

NORTH AMERICA

Osprey Direct, c/o Random House Distribution Center,
400 Hahn Road, Westminster, MD 21157, USA
E-mail: info@ospreydirect.com

ALL OTHER REGIONS

Osprey Direct UK, PO Box 140 Wellingborough, Northants, NN8 2FA, UK
E-mail: info@ospreydirect.co.uk

www.ospreypublishing.com

F-4C Phantom II cover art

1Lts Ralph Wetterhahn and Jerry Sharp of the 555th TFS/
8th TFW shot down a 921st FR MiG-21 during
Operation *Bolo* on January 2, 1967. Formations of F-4Cs
simulated an F-105 strike, and as four "Fishbeds" popped
up out of a dense cloud base, Col Robin Olds fired an
AIM-9 Sidewinder at one of them, but his missiles failed
to guide correctly. 1Lt Wetterhahn, flying as Col Olds'
wingman in F-4C 63-7589, shot off an AIM-7 Sparrow
at it instead, and he later recalled, "Both my back-seater
Sharp and I, as well as the two pilots in the No 3 aircraft
(Hicks and Brune), saw the missile go all the way and
impact the jet, sawing its tail clean off". This was the first
of seven MiG-21 kills during the brief, but decisive, *Bolo*
battle. No Phantom IIs were lost in return. (Artwork by
Gareth Hector)

MiG-21PFM cover art

Nguyen Tien Sam and his wingman, Nguyen Van Nghia,
of the 927th FR were vectored to an attack on "Bass"
flight of the 34th TFS/388th TFW on July 5, 1972. The
Phantom IIs were part of a 16-aircraft strike (equipped
with laser-guided bombs) sent to attack a target near Kep
airfield. Tien Sam and Van Nghia climbed out of thick
clouds just long enough to fire one "Atoll" missile each.
Nguyen Tien Sam's missile fatally damaged the F-4E flown
by Capt William Spencer and 1Lt Brian Seek (67-0296
"Bass 02"). Seconds later, another of the F-4Es (67-0339),
flown by Maj William Elander and 1Lt Don Logan, was
also hit. All four Phantom II aircrew became PoWs.
(Artwork by Gareth Hector)

Acknowledgments

I would like to thank the following individuals for their
assistance with this book – Dr István Toperczer, Attila
Mates (Czech Air Force), Ben Backes, Larry Hatcher,
Chris Hobson, Maj Gen Don Logeman, USAF (Ret.),
Capt M. A. Marshall, USAF (Ret), Col Bill McDonald,
USAF (Ret), Capt Fred Olmsted, USAF (Ret), Maj Gen
Dick Pascoe, USAF (Ret.), Peter Schinkelshoek, Lt Col
Fred Sheffler, USAF (Ret), Col James T. Talley, USAF
(Ret), Norm Taylor, Col Ralph Wetterhahn, USAF (Ret.)
and Brig Gen David O. Williams, USAF (Ret.). The text
also draws on correspondence and conversations with the
late Brig Gen Robin Olds, to whose memory this work is
dedicated.

CONTENTS

INTRODUCTION

In the peace deal following the end of French colonial rule in Vietnam in 1955, the country was divided at the 17th parallel. Since it was clear that the Viet Cong guerrillas operating in the South had full support from North Vietnam, it was inevitable that the USA, propping up South Vietnam, would have to cut off their supplies from the North. US ground troops began to arrive in December 1964, but air strikes were a more immediate method of attack. They were triggered by North Vietnamese attacks on US installations, leading first to Operation *Rolling Thunder* in 1965.

A series of limited air strikes was regarded as a better way to persuade the Hanoi government to disengage. In fact, it had quite the opposite effect.

Intense patriotism inspired the fledgling Vietnamese Peoples' Air Force (VPAF). Its pilots endured years of instruction from unpopular Russian mentors as they learned to fly the 65 MiG-17s that they had been given. Although their aircraft were a generation behind the American F-4 Phantom IIs and F-105s, they learned to use the simple jet's manoeuvrability and heavy guns to exploit the weaker areas of the sophisticated Western fighters' performance envelopes. The arrival of a few MiG-21s in late 1965 provided the USAF with a more credible opponent, although it was well into 1966 before VPAF pilots had mastered the supersonic fighters and learned appropriate strategies.

When air attacks began, the North relied mainly on its 1500 anti-aircraft guns, but soon incorporated Russian "Barlock" and "Flatface" early-warning radars to give fighters from their two jet-capable airfields the chance to intercept incoming American strikes.

Assuming that Hanoi would realise the folly of flouting the increasing threat of US air power after a few strikes, President Lyndon Johnson's government advocated a policy of "gradualism" in attacking targets of increasing strategic value, but stopping short of a series of decisive blows.

F-4 Phantom II pilots were also hamstrung by tight, constantly varying, Rules of Engagement. The most irksome for those who escorted bombing strikes was the requirement to identify enemy aircraft targets visually, rather than relying on the radar in their jets, which was designed to give them the advantage of firing their long-range missiles before the enemy could attack with guns or short-range missiles.

A USAF Project CHECO (Contemporary Historical Evaluation of Combat Operations) report later in the war pointed out that "on several occasions US fighters found that by the time visual identification of the MiG had been made they were no longer in the prescribed missile launch or range envelopes. The engagement then became a short-range manoeuvring encounter which further compounded the problem of accurate missile launch."

This requirement was introduced at the start of the war, and was barely relaxed even in the latter stages when better means of identification were available.

Once it was established, the pattern of strikes by formations of USAF and US Navy aircraft (each service having its own areas of responsibility, or "Route Packages") was almost unvaried throughout the war. USAF Phantom IIs were sent out as flights of four to accompany the bomber "packages" and to protect them from MiGs. Although the vast majority of US losses on those raids were attributed to anti-aircraft fire or SAMs, VPAF fighters, particularly MiG-21s, were seen as a significant threat. They usually appeared in very small numbers, if they appeared at all, but their effect in disrupting a bomber formation and forcing it to jettison its war load and defend itself was out of all proportion to the size of the MiG-21 force.

The prospect of shooting down an enemy aircraft in combat is central to any fighter pilot's ambitions, and it also attracts considerable propaganda importance. Although the aerial conflicts over North Vietnam were regarded even by fighter leader Col Robin Olds as a small part of the war, they were a powerful and visible focus for the rivalry and professionalism of the opposing forces.

The air war in Vietnam was mainly a "bombing war" for USAF Phantom II crews, although they had to be ready to face MiGs on any mission "up north." This 8th TFW F-4D at Ubon RTAFB is being loaded with "slick" bombs from an MJ-1 "jammer" vehicle, but it also carries an SUU-32/A gun pod, AIM-7E missiles and an AIM-4D Falcon (on its inner pylon). The 497th TFS "Night Owls'" emblem is just visible above the nose-gear door.

CHRONOLOGY

1946

July 21 McDonnell's first production aircraft, FH-1 Phantom, becomes first American jet to operate from an aircraft carrier. It is followed by F2H Banshee (March 1949) and F3H Demon (March 1956).

1954

October US Navy issues letter of intent for F3H-G, based on F3H Demon.

1955

Feb 14 MiG-OKB pilot G. K. Mosolov flies Ye-2 prototype, first in a series leading to MiG-21.

June 16 Grigory A. Sedov flies Ye-4, a Ye-2 with delta wings.

1958

May 8 Revised design, now F4H-1 prototype, rolled out, and it flies on May 27.

May 20 Testing begins for Ye-6, pre-production MiG-21.

1959

Oct 31 First speed record for Ye-66 (Ye-6/3). First deliveries of MiG-21F begin.

December F4H-1 begins series of record-breaking flights.

1960

Dec 29 F4H-1 enters US Navy service.

1962

Jan 24 Two F4H-1s are delivered to USAF as F-110As for evaluation and training.

1963

Feb 4 USAF Phantom II training begins, using 29 F-110As.

Nov 20 First USAF F-4C delivered.

1964

December First operational USAF F-4 unit, 12th TFW, deploys its 555th TFS to Okinawa. Whole wing deploys to Cam Ranh Bay, South Vietnam, November 8, 1965.

1965

March 2 First air strikes of *Rolling Thunder*, continuing until October 1968.

April 4 45th TFS/15th TFW, detached to Ubon RTAFB, flies first F-4C combat sorties, claiming first MiG-17 kill on July 10.

November Sixteen MiG-21F-13s are delivered to 921st FR "Sao Do" from Russia.

1966

January 921st FR commences VPAF operations with MiG-21F-13.

March 4 First "Atoll" kill (a Firebee drone) by MiG-21.

March 10 USAF F-4D deliveries begin. Aircraft replaces F-4C in Vietnam from Spring 1967 onwards.

April First MiG-21PF deliveries to VPAF.

April 23 First combat interception of F-4s by MiG-21s.

April 26 First MiG-21 claim by F-4C crew.

Oct 5 921st FR claims its first Phantom II destroyed (a US Navy F-4B).

1967

Jan 2 Operation *Bolo*. USAF claims seven MiG-21s but VPAF admits five losses. After this, MiG-21s retire from combat until April 23.

Jan 8 At VPAF tactics "summit" conference new tactics are agreed, using MiG-21s for slashing attacks that avoid long engagements with US fighters.

Two R-3S-armed MiG-21PFs man the alert at Noi Bai in August 1967. In the foreground, the pilot is being helped with his seat straps. His aircraft was amongst the first "Fishbed-Ds" delivered to the VPAF in April 1968.

June 5   First of 45 F-4D MiG kills is scored, the largest number for any F-4 variant.

1968
Nov 17   F-4Es deployed to Korat RTAFB.

1971
Oct 4   MiG-21s are detached to Dong Hoi, close to demilitarized zone, to attempt interception of incoming B-52s.
Nov 20   In first attempted interception of a B-52, Vu Dinh Rang claims his missile damaged a bomber.

1972
January   All 921st FR pilots flying MiG-21MF, and a few trained for night and bad weather operations.
Feb 3   Second MiG-21 unit, 927th FR "Lam Son," is formed with MiG-21PFM.
Feb 21   Combat with MiG-21s recommences, bringing first of 49 MiG kills.
May   Most new MiG-21 pilots train on MiG-21MF. Twelve train for B-52 interception.
May 9   Operation *Linebacker I* begins.
Autumn   Just 47 of 187 VPAF MiG-21s are operational on six bases, with 31 more stored to escape *Linebacker* raids.
December *Linebacker II* ends.

1973
Jan 7   4th TFS/432nd TRW F-4D crew make the final MiG-21 kill of the war.
Spring   MiG-21 units are re-deployed to new bases ahead of March 1975 "liberation" of South Vietnam by the North.

The F-4C-17-MC in the foreground first flew on December 18, 1963, and it was later converted into a prototype YF-4E to help with the development of the "gun-nose" Phantom II. The first F-4Cs in Vietnam wore this "Navy" gull gray and white color scheme.

DESIGN AND DEVELOPMENT

F-4 PHANTOM II

James Smith McDonnell founded his aircraft company in 1939 after several years as a designer for the Glenn Martin Company. Initially a subcontractor helping larger manufacturers such as Douglas fulfil World War II defense orders, he made enough money out of producing parts for C-47 Skytrains and A-20 Havocs to build a large factory at St Louis, in Missouri, in which he planned to produce his own designs.

On January 1, 1943, McDonnell was told to begin work on the US Navy's first carrier-borne jet, and within two years he had commenced delivering 60 FH-1 Phantom fighters, followed by larger-scale production of the bigger F2H Banshee fighter-bomber in 1949. The latter jet saw combat in the Korean War, and variants were developed for photo-reconnaissance, night/all-weather (with radar) and nuclear strike. McDonnell learned with the F2H that growth potential and adaptability made for a successful design – a lesson well expressed in the F-4 Phantom II.

The twin-engined Banshee was followed into US Navy service by the swept-wing F3H Demon interceptor, which featured a large search radar, four guns and four Sperry AAM-N-7 radar-guided missiles. It was McDonnell's only production aircraft to feature a single engine and, sadly, the chosen powerplant in the shape of the Westinghouse J40 was a dismal failure that seriously delayed the whole program. Re-engined Demons subsequently served with a small number of US Navy squadrons from 1956 to 1964. Once again, valuable lessons were learned for the F-4 programme.

A parallel design, the F-101 Voodoo, brought McDonnell its first big USAF contracts for bomber-escort, fighter and photo-reconnaissance versions of this big, twin-engined supersonic type. Conscious of the mixed fortunes of the F3H Demon, and anxious to secure US Navy business after the latter had contracted Vought to supply it with F-8 Crusader supersonic day fighters, McDonnell's designers were told to commence work on an unsolicited design for a twin-engined Demon successor (the F3H-G/H) in 1953. The US Navy duly obliged with an order for two prototypes from this very vague proposal (unlike the Soviet procurement process for the MiG-21).

Gradually, McDonnell designers refined their paper project until it had ten pylons for a huge ordnance load and, for a time, was designated the AH-1 attack fighter. However, the all-weather/nightfighter role was also kept very much in mind too by McDonnell so as to allow the jet to meet naval demands. David Lewis and Herman Barkey were placed in charge of the project, and they devised two versions – one with British (J65) Sapphire engines and the other using General Electric J79s, (a USAF-sponsored supersonic turbojet fitted in the F-104 Starfighter and B-58 Hustler).

As the F3H-G/H progressed, though still in something of a design vacuum, Barkey sketched various versions with interchangeable nose sections containing guns and rockets, or reconnaissance equipment. By April 1955 it became clear that the US Navy wanted a fleet defense fighter, and that announcement re-focused the design as the F4H-1. It was to perform three-hour combat air patrols (CAP) for the fleet using an eight-missile war-load to fend off intruders. Twin engines (a normal US Navy requirement for safety over water) would also enable one to be shut down for prolonged patrols.

A second crewman would be required to operate the complex electronic equipment and armament. The latter centered upon the long-range, semi-active radar controlled Raytheon Sparrow III missile, which allowed the fighter to detect threats well outside the fleet's defensive perimeter and destroy them at a considerable distance, without having to resort to dogfighting with guns or free-flight rockets. Interestingly though, a back-up gun still appeared in the plans until April 1957. Guidance was provided by a very large I/J-band search radar, with continuous wave injection to set the missiles on course and communicate with them until they could home onto the target using their own miniature radars.

The APQ-72 radar's 32-inch antenna eventually replaced the 24-inch version (and APQ-50 radar, as used in the F3H Demon and F4H prototypes) originally specified for the F4H-1 to give the Navy its desired detection range. It also changed the F4H-1's nose profile from the sharper shape of the prototypes to the familiar bulbous droop of production aircraft, and required the largest fibreglass radome ever made for a fighter. This was produced by the Brunswick Company, better known for its fibreglass boats and bowling balls. The flat profile of the low-drag cockpit canopy also had to be raised to improve visibility over the fatter nose.

Seven F4H-1s were ordered in July 1955, leaving McDonnell 30 months to turn its paper proposals into flying hardware. Many innovations were introduced, not least the variable geometry air intake system (the first in a fighter) and McDonnell's convergent/divergent afterburner nozzles, the latter making for smooth operation at high speeds rather than the "big bang" light-up synonymous with earlier units.

The most visible differences between the first prototype F4H-1 (seen here on an early flight in May 1958) and USAF F-4Cs were the larger radome, raised canopy and cutback air intakes of the production aircraft.

OPPOSITE
Probably the most famous USAF Phantom II of them all, F-4D-29-MC 66-7463 was responsible for shooting down five MiG-21s and a MiG-19. It is depicted here as it appeared on August 28, 1972 – the day that brought Capt Steve Ritchie ace status with his fifth kill and WSO Capt Chuck DeBellevue his fourth victory. Delivered new to the USAF on January 28, 1967, this aircraft served with units in the US, Japan and Thailand before being retired in October 1986. It was subsequently placed on permanent display in the grounds of the USAF Academy in Colorado Springs.

McDonnell aerodynamicist Art Lambert found that a very large vertical stabilizer gave the required directional stability at such high speeds. The F4H-1's "big tail" came about as a result of wind-tunnel tests rather than prototype flight testing, McDonnell accessing new materials like lightweight honeycomb structures to build parts of the Phantom II's tail. A stability augmentation system took a lot of the effort out of keeping the aircraft stable in the air.

Other radical features included outer wing panels that canted up 12 degrees to compensate for the slight negative dihedral in the main wing structure. The stabilator was given a 23-degree negative dihedral that aerodynamically complemented the wing dihedral for better roll stability. The F4H was thereby given an appearance which gave rise to the famous "delivered upside-down" quips when people first saw its drooping nose and oddly-angled flying surfaces. Lambert and Barkey had explored many configurations before building two prototypes, the first of which was ready to fly on May 27, 1958.

Test pilot Robert Little reached Mach 1.68 on the aircraft's third flight, and soon afterwards James McDonnell decided to call his new product "Phantom II," rather than "Satan" or "Ghost" as his employees preferred.

Vought was given the chance to compete with the F4H-1 with a fail-safe development of their Crusader, designated the F8U-3. Although the latter demonstrated superior performance in many areas, the US Navy opted for the security of two seats, two engines and more versatile armament capability. It was also impressed by the boundary-layer control system, inspired by a similar system in the F8U-3, which improved landing characteristics. Deliveries of production F4H-1s began in February 1961 after the aircraft had set three world speed and altitude records (it went on to smash another dozen by April 12, 1962), and in September 1962 it was re-designated F-4B.

The USAF's first Phantom IIs (a pair of borrowed F4H-1s) were handed over as F-110As on January 24, 1962. Subsequently joined by 27 other F-110As, they began flying with the 4453rd Combat Crew Training Wing at McDill AFB, Florida. When

F-4D PHANTOM II

58ft 2.4in.

16ft 6in.

38ft 5in.

purpose-built F-4Cs with "minimum change" USAF modifications to their undercarriage, in-flight refuelling system and avionics began to arrive, they formed two fighter wings, the 12th TFW (operational by October 1964) and the 15th TFW. Both deployed to Southeast Asia in 1965, where the 45th TFS/15th TFW scored the first F-4C MiG kills.

The USAF purchase of a naval design was a tribute to the Phantom II's performance, and took into account the ordnance-carrying capability that remained in the airframe after the US Navy switched its interest in the type from attack to interception in 1955. It was also facilitated by US Secretary of Defense Robert S. McNamara, whose controversial policy of "commonality" required the armed forces to share technology in order to save money. Although this ran into severe difficulties in his flagship F-111 program, it led to successes like the A-7 Corsair II and F-4 Phantom II.

For the USAF Phantom II, its reconnaissance RF-4C variant and the F-4D and F-4E all shared components with the US Navy's F-4J and US Marine Corps' RF-4B. By 1967, the F-4 had been issued to two-thirds of the USAF's tactical fighter wings, and the development of follow-on variants continued apace.

Some of the basic design problems inherited by the USAF when it adopted the F-4C/D for service posed difficulties for air and groundcrews during the war. For example, when designing the jet's AN/ARC-105 HF radio, Collins Radio Corporation had had to find a solution to the electromagnetic interference that adversely affected its equipment. It also struggled with the placement of antennas within the airframe. For example, the forward area of skin on the vertical stabilizer was used for a high frequency antenna, and in a manoeuvring fight this could be blanked off by other parts of the aircraft, interrupting transmissions.

The fighter's avionics also proved unsuited to the heat and humidity of Southeast Asia, with sealing compounds degenerating rapidly, causing electrical insulation problems. The radio was particularly susceptible to water leakage into the cockpit, and repair or maintenance of this equipment, or its associated battery, required removal of the rear ejection seat – an awkward and potentially risky task.

The introduction of the F-4D Phantom II brought some improvements in bombing capability and a partially solid-state radar. F-4D-30-MC 66-7554 has one star for the last MiG kill of *Rolling Thunder* (using a gun pod) and a second one transferred from another aircraft or pilot. *TRAPPER* carries a combat camera in place of one AIM-7 and a full load of "slick" bombs fitted with fuse extenders to make them detonate above ground level.

By 1972, all F-4s heading North needed to carry vital bolt-on ECM equipment like the two AN/ALQ-101(V)-1 pods seen here. They took up weapons space, in this case the forward missile troughs on 13th TFS F-4D-31-MC 66-7680. Yet even the presence of these pods provided no guarantee of safety, as this aircraft was destroyed by a SAM on July 5, 1972 – the same day that two 388th TFW F-4Es were shot down during a lightning MiG-21 attack. Vectored through low cloud, Nguyen Tien Sam and his wingman popped up through the undercast, fired their missiles and dived away, leaving the two F-4s in flames and four more names for the growing PoW list.

The lack of a back-up radio was also criticised by pilots, who had to change channels constantly in battle so as to monitor a multiplicity of inputs from different sources, including in-cockpit intercom conversation, and then try to prioritize them. A small separate receiver gave them "Guard" channel, which accepted SAM and MiG warnings, but this was often saturated by the incessant interference from rescue "beepers" activated by downed aircrew.

A small panel by the pilot's right knee (or the back-seater's left knee) had "comm freq" and "comm chan" controls that allowed the crew to rapidly change radio frequencies, but important information could nevertheless be missed if a pilot happened to be on the wrong channel, or missed a "channel change" signal from his flight leader, thereby losing touch with his flight. Complete radio failure – the so-called "nordo" situation – also frequently happened.

A far more serious situation arose from the F-4's naval interceptor background in terms of its armament. Naval Aviators flying the F-4B anticipated carefully prepared, long-range interceptions in which both aircrew had time to tune their radar and missiles and achieve a "full-systems lock-on," where all parts of the radar/Constant Wave guidance/missile chain were properly employed. Their theoretical targets would be large, non-maneuvering aircraft at medium or high altitude, offering no opposition. In Vietnam the same system could work well, given similar conditions, but these were all too rare. Far more often the aircrew would have brief notice of their intended target, little time to "prime" the systems and a small, violently maneuvering target that had ample notice of their presence and every intention of effectively fighting back.

The F-4C/D's missiles were controlled by a row of switches situated on a small panel at the lower left edge of the main instrument display. The third small switch in the row had three positions – "up" for AIM-7 Sparrow, "middle" for AIM-9 Sidewinder and "down" to sequence through the latter missiles to find the one with the best seeker tone. Doing this accurately involved looking down into the cockpit – disastrous for the pilot's situational awareness in combat, and a great way to lose sight of a small target like a MiG-21. Some pilots fitted bits of plastic tubing to the switch to make it easier to judge its position while wearing gloves.

Since it was often impossible to allow time for a full radar lock-on, or too difficult to maintain the correct range parameters from the target to do so, pilots often resorted to "boresight" mode – essentially "slaving" the radar to the gunsight. MiG-killer Col Terry Talley explained:

> The F-4 radar was very difficult to use in its standard mode. We had serious problems getting a radar lock on a maneuvering target that then allowed the missile to be launched. As a solution to our issues with the APQ-72, the radars in our jets were modified so that with a flick of a switch they could be slaved in azimuth and elevation to the nose of the aircraft, creating a narrow, forward-pointing beam. This simplified the process, since all the aircraft commander (front-seater) had to do was point the F-4 at the target and it would appear in the radar beam.

In "full-systems" mode, it was necessary to maintain radar contact with the target until the missile hit it. During that time the F-4 was unable to maneuver or avoid attack by another MiG – an entirely unsatisfactory situation for the crew of a fighter aircraft that was not resolved until the 1990s with the development of the AIM-120 AMRAAM medium range "launch and leave" missile.

MiG-21

The evolution of the MiG-21 and the F-4 Phantom II took place in roughly the same time period, but they had very different origins. When the Mikoyan-Gurevich Ye-6s (essentially pre-production MiG-21s) began test flying on May 20, 1958, they were the culmination of a series of five development types dating back to the Ye-2 in February 1955. The prefix "Ye" indicated "yedenitsa", or "one-off." The program aimed to produce a supersonic, land-based, single-seat point-defense day fighter to protect Russian military installations from high-flying bombers.

McDonnell's Phantom II originated from US Navy requirements issued in 1954, but no flying hardware appeared until the prototype took to the sky for the first time on May 8, 1958. This aircraft was designed to provide worldwide, long-range fleet defense, using its radar-guided missiles to keep attacking aircraft at bay, or its enormous ordnance-carrying capacity to support carrier-based bombers in the attack role. At that time, few could have foreseen any reason why, a decade later, these two very different types would be fighting it out in a desperate aerial conflict over a small southeast Asian country.

The fighters' main design differences sprang partly from their armament. American interception techniques in the 1950s used collision-course guidance in which the fighter approached a target from the front, having first detected it with a powerful radar. Long-range missiles would then be fired, avoiding the need for closer combat. However, if that attack method failed and the fighter was fast enough (speed was not crucial for a head-on attack), it would turn in behind the target and make a second

attempt using shorter-range heat-seeking missiles or guns. This was the Phantom II's original mission profile.

Lacking sophisticated radars and missiles, Soviet MiGs at that time relied upon speed to pursue their targets, firing short-range missiles or heavy-caliber cannon when in range.

US interception techniques required a large aircraft that could contain enough fuel for long patrols, carry a heavy load of eight missiles and feature a second seat for a radar operator. The jet also had to feature two engines, thus satisfying the US Navy's requirement for better safety margins in over-water operations.

The MiG-21's role demanded a lightweight, short-range, single-seater that was capable of reaching its target at supersonic speed and destroying it with minimal gun or missile armament. Whereas one Phantom II could theoretically destroy six intruders in a single sortie, units equipped with lightly armed MiG-21s would have to rely on large numbers to negate a substantial threat.

Both fighters were heavily influenced by the aerial dogfighting of the Korean War, which had seen the first jet-versus-jet engagements between the MiG-15 and F-86 Sabre. Both fighters possessed similar performance, but superior USAF training had allowed the American units to prevail.

At the same time that the swirling dogfights of the Korean War were taking place, the Soviet air force (VVS) was specifying a requirement for a much faster fighter to take on the USAF's F-100 Super Sabre and B-47 and B-52 bombers. The advent of the supersonic B-58 Hustler bomber added Mach 2 speed at 65,000ft to the list of potential threat aircraft that the VVS needed to oppose. Rapid rate of climb and high maneuverability were paramount, but night or all-weather capability was not required.

Included in the first batch of "Fishbeds" delivered to the VPAF, MiG-21F-13 4520 was flown by eight-kill ace Pham Thanh Ngan. He claimed an RF-101C downed whilst flying it on September 16, 1967. The veteran fighter has been on display in the Thai Nguyen Military District museum for many years. An example of an early MiG-21F was passed on to the USAF by the Israeli government after Iraqi pilot Capt Munir Radfa defected with it to Israel in August 1966. It was secretly tested at Groom Lake in Project *Have Donut*, when US pilots found it hard to maneuver below 210kts and above 510kts. Below 12,000ft, the jet's fuel pumps could not deliver enough fuel to the engine when in full afterburner, limiting speed to around 590kts.

OPPOSITE
MiG-21PFM 5015 of the 921st
FR "Sao Do" in 1972 was one
of a number of MiG-21s that
had random camouflage
patterns thinly painted over
their aluminium finish. A few
appeared in various shades of
blue or gray, others in overall
green or blotchy green
patterns. The camouflage
worked well for MiGs making
zoom-climb attacks from low
altitude, or to disguise them
if they were forward deployed
to airfields that were highly
vulnerable to US air strikes.

Like other contemporary Soviet fighters, the new contender had to be simple in construction and undemanding on maintenance (unlike the Phantom II).

In the spring of 1953, the MiG OKB (experimental aircraft design bureau) was instructed to produce a lightweight, supersonic interceptor, while the rival Sukhoi OKB proceeded with heavier, radar-equipped, all-weather fighters that were more akin to the Phantom II concept. Several very different MiG prototypes were built following the wind-tunnel testing of models that tried out a range of possible configurations in the air. The first, designated the Ye-2, had sharply swept wings and a tail unit like the MiG-19. Spin-off prototypes included the Ye-50 with dual jet and rocket power like the projected British Saunders-Roe SR 177 interceptor. Gradually, the Ye-2 evolved into the MiG-23, although not the later variable-geometry MiG-23 "Flogger."

The other configuration, flight-tested as the Ye-4, used a delta (referred to as a "balalaika" in Russia) wing attached to a Ye-2 fuselage. This flew on June 16, 1955, and quickly began to resemble the definitive MiG-21. Using a delta eased the application of the recently established "area rule" concept, which, by reducing "wave drag" over the fuselage, made supersonic flight more feasible. Unlike most contemporary Western delta-wing designs like the Vulcan, Mirage and F-102, the Russians gave their first delta a sharply-swept, all-moving horizontal tail. In comparative trials, the Ye-4 wing demonstrated slightly higher speed, better rate of roll and greater fuel capacity than the swept-wing Ye-2.

Great fighter designs rely on outstanding engine technology, and the team headed by S. K. Tumanskii, which had produced the afterburning RD-9 engine for the MiG-19, created the R-11. Despite being the same size as the RD-9, it yielded 50 per cent more thrust. The powerplant was installed in the Ye-5 – a modified Ye-4 with a new airbrake and three large fences above each wing to improve stability. The nose was lengthened, a bigger afterburner was installed and the engine proved ultimately proved successful, despite early fires and turbine failures.

Final prototypes, designated Ye-6s, were followed by ten pre-production MiG-21s built at the state Tbilisi plant. These had uprated RD-11F-300 engines, squared-off wingtips and two under-wing hard-points. Tail surfaces were enlarged, a single ventral fin replaced two smaller strakes and the air intake, with its three-position conical center-body, was modified to improve airflow at high angles of attack. The front-hinged cockpit canopy, inspired by the British Folland Gnat, was strengthened, though not enough to save test pilot Vladimir Nefyedov when the Ye-6 prototype he was flying crashed inverted after an engine flameout.

As development progressed, the wing fences were reduced to two smaller examples and two 30mm NR-30 guns, each fed by a 30-round belt, were added in the underfuselage below the wing roots. The third Ye-6 tested the centerline fuel tank, which added 400 miles to the aircraft's range at altitude.

In late 1958 research centre OKB-134 was told to produce a copy of an American AIM-9B Sidewinder missile – an example of the latter had been acquired from China as a misfired trophy after scraps with Nationalist Chinese fighters near Taiwan. The copy, dubbed R-3S, was ready for testing in February 1959, and Ye-6/2 was modified to carry two on wing-tip launchers like the F-104 and F-5. Poor test results changed

MiG-21PFM

48ft 2.75in.

13ft 5.5in.

23ft 5.5in.

their location to the two under-wing hard-points on APU-13 launchers. This simple armament configuration at least made for quick turn-around times – an early MiG-21 could be rearmed and have its fuel topped up inside ten minutes.

The third prototype Ye-6/3 masqueraded as the "Ye-66" and established world records for absolute speed (October 1959) and 100km closed circuit speed (September 1960), reaching a maximum speed of 1,556mph. For production MiG-21s, the possibility of Mach 2 speed was severely curtailed by the aircraft's limited fuel capacity.

Based on the Ye-6T, the MiG-21F ("F" for "Forsazh" or "boosted") entered production at Gorkiy in 1958, with the first deliveries of 40 aircraft made in the autumn of 1959. Like early variants of many aircraft, this was the lightest, simplest and most easily flown MiG-21 model of them all. As extra equipment and, consequently, weight were added to later versions, it became harder to handle.

This process began with the next version, the MiG-21F-13, which had extra fuel in integral wing-tanks and a centerline pylon for a drop tank. Unlike the F-4, no ordnance could be attached to this pylon. The left cannon was removed to accommodate guidance equipment for the two R-3S missiles. MiG-21F-13s were delivered to the VVS's first operational MiG-21 unit (28th Fighter Regiment) at Odessa in 1962. Final production configuration was not decided until the 115th example, after which a shorter, broader tail-fin was used.

The MiG-21PF ("P" stood for "perekhvatchik" or "interceptor"), which replaced the MiG-21F-13 in production from 1962, introduced important modifications, including an extension of the fin's leading edge to reduce yaw. A frequent problem afflicting supersonic aircraft, yaw could cause an engine stall if the aircraft was turned too abruptly at high speed. Combined with the need for a larger intake cone to house a search radar, thus making the aircraft a true interceptor, Mikoyan was forced to enlarge the intake, lengthen the nose and remove the remaining gun to preserve the centre of gravity.

The ASP-PF radar scope/sight system required a heavy-duty visor so that the pilot could see its rather dim CRT imagery. Concentrating on the scope obviously limited his awareness of other aspects of cockpit management, however. In the F-4 the "scope gazing" was done by the back-seater, whose role in USAF F-4s changed from "pilot"

Two MiG-21PFMs are scrambled from Noi Bai during the intense fighting of mid-May 1972. Both jets are armed with a pair of R-3S "Atoll" missiles, and lack centerline drop tanks. The absence of the latter indicate that the short-range "Fishbeds" have been sent aloft on an airfield defense mission. The MiG-21's small cross-section made it very hard to detect head-on. These jets would have been little more than tiny dots for a US pilot trying to spot them at a distance of two or three miles – only seconds away from missile launch range for the "Atoll."

to "weapons systems officer" (WSO). The front-seat aircraft commander had a repeater scope on his instrument panel. The "Spin Scan" radar in the MiG-21 was severely affected by ground clutter below 3,000ft, and the F-4C had similar problems that were later overcome in the US Navy's F-4J by the use of pulse Doppler technology.

The MiG-21PF's cockpit, unlike the Phantom II's, offered pilot protection. A 62mm-thick armoured glass panel was placed vertically above the main instrument panel, the seat head-rest was armoured and the metal of the cockpit walls was reinforced.

Both the MiG-21 and F-4 had hydraulic flight controls with traditional push-pull rods to operate their power control units, although the Phantom II's stability-augmentation equipment (giving similar results to early fly-by-wire systems) took much of the labour out of operating the controls. The MiG-21's control column was much longer than the F-4's, partly to overcome the heavy "stick forces" encountered in flight.

Engine starting was electrical, using a single "start" button. The F-4C/D had a spectacularly smoky cartridge starter system, but crews typically resorted to an external compressed air starter like their naval antecedents. Afterburner engagement was incorporated in the single-lever throttle system, rather than requiring movement of the throttles past a detent position as in the F-4. It was therefore smoothly integrated into the range of engine power settings, rather than as a separate operation. Internal fuel capacity of the MiG-21F-13 provided only 515 gallons of useable fuel, plus 108 gallons in the early "subsonic" drop tank. This compared with the F-4C's total fuel load, with three external tanks, of 3,365 gallons – in itself a graphic indication of the two fighters' different design philosophies.

MiG-OKB was under constant pressure to produce radical modifications of its designs to rival Western developments, such as an aircraft suitable for short-field runway operations for which the bureau devised a ski undercarriage for the Ye-5. The Ye-8 tested canard fore-planes, a "chin" air intake and an extra 200 gallons of internal

A MiG-21UM "Mongol-B" two-seat trainer of the 927th FR heads up a row of 921st FR MiG-21MF "Fishbed-Js" at Noi Bai in the spring of 1972.

fuel. There was even a short take-off variant with two additional lift engines, designated the 23-31. The Ye-7 prototypes tested various reconnaissance pods, flap-blowing systems (included in the MiG-21PFS and later variants), the SRU-2M IFF (identification friend or foe) transponder and the two spine-mounted additional fuel tanks that became a feature of the MiG-21PF, although they added only another 81 gallons. A third 66-gallon tank was added in the MiG-21SMT, but later removed when it was found to cause stability and drag problems. A number of VPAF MiG-21s were lost due to fuel starvation.

The MiG-21 quickly proved to be a tough, reliable machine. The quality of some of its components did not match Western standards at first – tyre life was short, and some airframe parts needed frequent replacement, but it was generally easy to maintain. However, none of the later versions in VPAF service cured the problem of very limited forward vision for the pilot or inadequate fuel capacity. The type's basic power-to-weight ratio meant that substantial improvements to the MiG-21 were inevitably limited, despite the huge number of sub-variants that were built. In direct contrast, many F-4s, towards the end of their careers, had accumulated over 1,000lbs in weight just in airframe reinforcement without significantly affecting performance.

The MiG-21bis, which entered VVS service in late 1972 and was beginning to appear within the ranks of the VPAF at the end of the war, was in many ways the apex of the aircraft's development. Its new R-25-300 engine offered much-improved afterburning, which boosted the aircraft's performance at low altitudes and allowed it to attain Mach 1 at sea level. The GSh-23L gun was built into the airframe, with its 200-round ammunition belt wrapped around the air intake ducting. Although, externally at least, the MiG-21bis resembled early versions of the "Fishbed," two decades of development and structural change made it a very different aircraft.

Although not strictly from the Vietnam War period, MiG-21bis "Fishbed-L" 5236 is representative of the aircraft delivered to the VPAF in the final weeks of the *Linebacker II* offensive. Put on display in Hanoi's Lenin Square, this aircraft has been painted in two shades of gray. It saw active service with the 921st Fighter Regiment at Noi Bai.

TECHNICAL
SPECIFICATIONS

USAF F-4 PHANTOM II

F-4C

This first USAF variant was introduced as the F-110A until the 1962 designation changes that saw it re-numbered the F-4C. McDonnell produced 583 F-4Cs, which was basically the US Navy's two-seat F-4B carrier-borne interceptor but with wider (30in. x 7.7in.) wheels and correspondingly thicker wing roots. A pop-up refuelling receptacle in the fuselage spine replaced the US Navy's extending probe and a cartridge-driven starting system was introduced.

In the rear cockpit, a control column, primary flight instruments and throttles were added, as the USAF considered this variant a "two pilot" fighter. This meant that the Phantom II could be used as a trainer (although landing it from the rear cockpit was hazardous), whereas MiG-21 pilots had to rely on the two-seat, purpose-built, MiG-21U trainer.

Because the F-4's rear cockpit was designed for a naval radar-scope watcher rather than for a pilot, the view was very restricted to the rear and downwards because of the air intakes. As pilot John Nash commented, "You could not see straight aft in a Phantom II at all. Internal canopy mirrors were of very limited use, and it was quite a while before the Israeli practice of fitting an external mirror to the center canopy bow was adopted."

The toughness inherent in a naval design contrasted with the more fragile structure of the MiG-21, although the F-4's hydraulic systems were very vulnerable to damage, even from small-arms fire. Additional USAF equipment included a Litton AN/ASQ-48 inertial navigation system and expanded weapons control panels, enabling delivery of all USAF tactical stores. The naval folding wings and massive tailhook were retained.

The F-4B's fleet defense role was based on an armament of four AIM-7D Sparrow III semi-active, radar-guided missiles with a range of 25 miles. Secondary armament, in the unlikely event of closer combat with intruding bombers, was a quartet of infrared-seeking AIM-9B Sidewinders with a 2.6-mile range. This missile combination was retained, with updates, on all successive variants (apart from the reconnaissance optimized RF-4C Phantom II).

Sparrow targets were located and initial guidance provided by a big Westinghouse APQ-100 I/J–band interception radar in the bulbous radome – a more reliable and capable unit than any used in MiG-21s of the time. The two GE J79 turbojets produced nearly two-and-a-half times the thrust of the MiG-21's single engine in a fighter with only twice the MiG's weight. This conferred a stellar rate of climb (derived from the naval interception role), which gave Phantom II pilots the advantage in a vertical fight. From 1965, the lack of an internal gun could be partially remedied by strapping an M61A1 Vulcan rotary cannon in an SUU-16/A pod onto the center pylon.

The F-4C/D's radios were often criticized. In designing the AN/ARC-105 HF radio, Collins Radio Corporation struggled with electromagnetic interference and placement of antennas, particularly in the vertical tail. During maneuvering flight, the tail-mounted antenna could be blocked by the airframe, interrupting transmissions. Because aircraft avionics suffered in the humid tropical conditions of South-east Asia, repairs were common. In the F-4, rain leaking into the cockpit was channelled directly to the radio, and access to it, or its battery, meant removal of the rear seat – an unpopular and risky task for groundcrews.

F-4D

Reflecting McDonnell's confidence in the Phantom II, work began on the F-4D and the "recce" RF-4C variant while the C-model was still under test. In March 1966, the balance of the USAF's order for 1,342 F-4Cs was canceled in favor of the improved F-4D. Using the same airframe and engines, its improvements were concentrated in the attack mode so that Phantom IIs could replace the rapidly dwindling F-105 Thunderchiefs in battle – the F-4D was also a superior air-to-air fighter too. Its new AN/APQ-109 radar gave an air-to-air ranging mode, with moveable cursors operating in conjunction with an AN/ASQ-91 automatic weapons release computer system for much more accurate bombing, particularly in "dive-toss" mode from high altitude.

The F-4C's crude fixed gunsight was replaced by an AN/ASG-22 lead-computing optical sight set, and the aircraft was also equipped to employ the new generations of optically-guided and "smart" weapons that were just entering frontline service. Less satisfactory was the decision by the USAF to replace the US Navy-initiated Sidewinder with its "own" AIM-4D Falcon IR-homing missile. In combat use, this weapon proved unreliable and complex, scoring only five kills ("as useless as tits on a boar-hog" was how Robin Olds described it to this author). *Red Baron* said it had the most complex firing process of any US missile. Despite partial success, initiated by Col Olds, in reinstating the AIM-9, many F-4Ds retained the Falcon until after Vietnam. An improved gun pod in the form of the SUU-23/A could also be carried. A total of 793 F-4Ds were acquired by the USAF.

A version of the QRC-248 IFF interrogator as used in the EC-121 airborne early warning aircraft was installed in eight F-4Ds as APX-81 *Combat Tree*. They deployed to Udorn RTAFB in December 1971, and the jets became such valuable assets thanks to their ability to identify MiGs for AIM-7 firing well beyond visual range that another 20 were converted.

This well worn F-4C-21-MC (64-0841) belonged to the 433rd TFS/8th TFW "Wolfpack," and it is seen here upon its return to Ubon RTAFB with empty multiple ejector bomb racks and FFAR rocket pods in the summer of 1967.

F-4 PHANTOM II MISSILE ARMAMENT

When configured for MiGCAP, F-4Ds and F-4Es usually carried a pair of AIM-7E/E-2 Sparrow IIIs in their rear missile wells. One or both of the forward missile wells could be occupied by an ECM pod or strike camera. The inner wing pylons carried AIM-9E/J Sidewinders (or AIM-4D Falcons on some F-4Ds), plus AN/ALQ-87 or AN/ALQ-101 ECM pods.

F-4E GUN ARMAMENT

The General Electric M61A1 20mm "Gatling" cannon, used by the F-4E and many other US fighters, employed a rotating, hydraulically powered, six-barrel system. This permitted a 6,000 rounds per minute rate of fire, and also lengthened barrel life and reduced overheating. A large ammunition drum held 639 rounds of linkless ammunition. Spent shell cases were returned to the drum. The whole package weighed 1,028lbs, and could be removed for maintenance.

F-4E

Phantom II crews' experiences during *Rolling Thunder* persuaded the Pentagon that an internal gun should be added to the F-4. F-105s had scored 23 MiG kills using the M61A1 rotary cannon, and gun pod toting F-4C/Ds added another ten in situations where missiles had either failed or were outside launch parameters. The F-4E – the "definitive" USAF Phantom II – entered squadron service on October 3, 1967, and units equipped with the aircraft started flying combat operations over Vietnam two years later. In all, 865 were delivered to the USAF out of 1,100 produced. In effect, the USAF took over the US Navy's F-4 project, buying three times as many Phantom IIs.

In addition to the nose-mounted gun, the aircraft had J79-GE-17C engines, up-rated to 17,900lbs maximum thrust. However, like previous J79s, the engines still emitted thick black smoke-trails except when in afterburner. This made the aircraft visible for up to 30 miles. Fixes were developed but never implemented during the war.

An extra fuel cell was added in the rear fuselage, partly to balance the longer nose. The new nose was adopted following the fitment of the lighter, more compact AN/APQ-120 solid-state radar and antenna, which was heavily insulated against

This LORAN-equipped F-4D carries a single AIM-4D Falcon missile as part of its ordnance. Despite its poor performance in *Rolling Thunder*, the Falcon was retained as the secondary armament for many F-4Ds during *Linebacker*, although it scored no MiG kills in 1972–73. The missile worked better when protected inside the ordnance bays of F-102 and F-106 interceptors, for its delicate sensors suffered weather attrition on the exposed F-4D pylons.

gunfire vibration. The AN/APQ-120 was slightly less long-ranging than the F-4D's AN/APQ-109 system.

In an effort to save weight, McDonnell Douglas deleted the seldom-used pop-out ram air turbine and the powered wing-folding mechanism. Finally, an F-4J-type slotted tailplane increased control effectiveness.

In November 1972, a squadron of *Rivet Haste* F-4Es arrived in Thailand for the final weeks of the air war, although they encountered no MiGs. These jets incorporated further improvements via fixed leading-edge slats to boost turn rate, stall characteristics and low-speed handling. Protruding from the left wing-root was a TISEO telescopic device, slaved to the radar for long-range visual target identification. APX-81 *Combat Tree* was also included, together with the long-desired "556" cockpit update which sorted out some of the random distribution of controls and instruments. Most air-to-air armament switches were clustered on the left throttle and ordnance controls were grouped on the upper left instrument panel so that pilots could manage their armament without taking their eyes off the external combat scenario.

Although the slats and the extra weight of the gun and No 7 fuel tank reduced maximum speed to below Mach 2, crews welcomed the new wing configuration, as it made the Phantom II almost spin-proof.

The F-4E marked the apex of USAF Phantom II development, particularly in its final slatted-wing configuration. This 388th TFW F-4E-34-MC (67-0269), seen at Korat RTAFB, has the original short gun muzzle fairing, and is carrying a mixed load of Mk 82 bombs and SUU-30 cluster bombs. The metal revetments, filled with blast-absorbing sand, contrasted sharply with the simple earth blast walls erected at MiG bases in 1967. The variations in camouflage between the jet in the foreground and the F-4E parked behind it are also noteworthy.

A hungry-looking SUU-23/A gun pod mounted beneath an F-4D. The earlier SUU-16/A lacked the intake above the nose of the pod. Korean War ace Col (later Maj Gen) "Boots" Blesse championed the SUU-16/A gun pod with the 366th TFW. "I thought we could take that SUU-16 to Hanoi and increase our air-to-air capability," he subsequently recalled.

MiG-21 (VPAF USE ONLY)

The MiG-21 has been produced in greater numbers and used by more air forces than any other post war combat aircraft apart from the C-130 Hercules. Around 10,000 were built, which was almost twice as many as the F-4 Phantom II. At the time of the first MiG-21F-13 deliveries to the VPAF it was still Russia's most effective interceptor. Exact figures for wartime deliveries to the VPAF are still classified in Vietnam, but they averaged about 40 annually. Of the 17 VPAF pilots claiming ace status, 13 flew MiG-21s.

MiG-21F-13 (TYPE 74) "FISHBED-C"

As the first mass-produced version of the MiG-21, and based on the Ye-6 prototypes, the "Fishbed-C" saw service from 1960 onwards. It also provided the basis for 17 subsequent variants, was the first MiG-21 to boast missile armament and the first to be exported. Its delta wing, swept at 57 degrees, had hydraulic flaps and boosted ailerons, with pylons for two R-3S (K-13) "Atoll" missiles. S-5 or S-24 free-flight rocket pods could also be carried, and these were sometimes used against US aircraft.

The weapons' basic range information came from a SRD-5M Kvant ("High Fix") radar-ranging device, housed in the air intake variable-position center body (one of the first examples of this type), and this was effective up to a range of four miles. It projected a very thin, fixed radar beam straight ahead of the aircraft and fed range data back to the gunsight. Unlike the Phantom II, there was no cockpit radar scope, merely an ASP-5D gyro gunsight linked to a display of indicator lights showing that the aircraft was at minimum (3,000ft) or maximum (2.5 miles) "Atoll" range. Often, pilots would follow up a missile launch with their single NR-30 gun (the second gun was removed to accommodate electronics associated with the "Atoll" missile).

The simple fuselage, only four feet in diameter, had two rear-mounted airbrakes, while much of its forward section was occupied by a split air duct that channeled air from the nose intake past the cockpit shell to the single, simple and tough engine. The entire rear section could be removed for engine servicing, as with the F-100 and F-105. One-piece, all-flying tailplanes, swept at 55 degrees, had distinctive tip-mounted anti-flutter mass balances. The hydraulic undercarriage retracted inwards into the fuselage. The cockpit canopy hinged forward, separating to protect the pilot in an ejection (only possible above an altitude of 360ft), although the interlock between the SK ejection seat and canopy release proved unreliable.

North Vietnam's MiG-21F-13s, like all export models, were made at the MMZ Znamaya Truda factory in Moscow between 1962–65. Their small profile and smoke-free engines made them difficult to detect, particularly from head-on. Phantom II pilots hoped to catch sun reflections off a canopy or natural metal surface. Some VPAF MiGs were camouflaged, but in an effort to reduce their visibility on the ground or over water, rather than in the air.

MiG-21PF (TYPE 76) "FISHBED-D"

This version had a more powerful R-11F-300 engine (14,307lbs max. thrust) that required a seven-inch increase in air intake diameter, which in turn accommodated a larger RP-21 Sapfir ("Spin Scan") search radar. The MiG-21F-13's rear canopy glazing was replaced by a dorsal fairing, increasing internal fuel to 726 gallons. An improved PKI-1 gunsight was installed, and this could be used in high-g maneuvers. However, no gun was fitted in keeping with the general replacement of guns with missiles in fighters at the time. Undercarriage wheels were larger and short take off-assisting SPRD-99 rocket pods could be attached to the rear fuselage. Production, at the Gorkiy plant, took place until 1968.

MiG-21 pilots relied on the R-3S "Atoll" for most of their engagements. Here, Nguyen Tien Sam checks the guidance "rollerons" of a missile fitted to his jet for free movement. Tien Sam claimed six kills with the 921st and 927th FRs from 1968–72, including F-4E 66-0369 on July 24, 1972. He was almost shot down by another Phantom II as he landed at Noi Bai shortly after the fight.

MiG-21PFS (TYPE 94) "FISHBED-E" AND MiG-21PFM "FISHBED-F"

These variants introduced blown (Atinello) flaps, inspired by their use in the F-4, to improve turn rate in combat and attempt to ease the MiG-21's notoriously demanding landing characteristics (high approach speeds). An obvious external difference was the side-hinged canopy and fixed, heavy-framed windshield, both of which further reduced the poor visibility for the pilot. Forward vision was severely impeded by the large gunsight, and there was a 50-degree "blind zone" behind the wing leading edge. Downward vision was limited by the high canopy rails and narrow glazing. Phantom II pilots were encouraged to attack in these blind areas.

Tail fin area was increased for better directional stability, and an improved KM-1 ejection seat was used. The drag parachute container, with a cross-shaped canopy, was moved from beneath the rear fuselage to the base of the vertical fin.

Armament included a pair of K-5M semi-active radar-homing missiles, guided by a new RP-21M radar (effective up to 15 miles) in a similar way to the AIM-7 Sparrow. Like the F-4D Phantom II, the MiG-21PFS had a centerline mounting that could take the weight of a gun pod, recessed in this instance, housing a very effective Gryasev-Shipunov twin-barrel 23mm GSh-23 cannon aimed through an ASP-PF-21 gunsight and giving about five seconds' firing time (200 rounds). The lower fuselage ahead of the line of fire had to be reinforced with a steel plate.

MiG-21 "ATOLL" MISSILE

Basic armament for the MiG-21 was a pair of R-3S "Atoll" infrared homing missiles, copied from the US AIM-9B Sidewinder. For the MiG-21MF and MiG-21bis, two extra wing pylons were provided.

MiG-21 CANNON POD

MiG-21F-13s had a single NR-30 cannon with 30 rounds (each of which weighed about a pound), but later "Fishbed" variants, as depicted here, could be fitted with the twin-barrel GSh-23 electrically fired cannon, capable of expending 3,600 rounds per minute, in a GP-9 removable pack.

Like US aircraft, the MiG-21PFM had a passive radar-ranging receiver ("Sirena-3M") to alert the pilot to "lock-ons" by hostile missiles.

The MiG-21PFS had a brief production run before being supplanted by the MiG-21PFM, which differed only in having a more controllable afterburner. Export models were produced between 1964–68. The MiG-21PFMA sub-variant had a larger tailfin like the MiG-21MF and provision for four under-wing pylons.

MiG-21MF (TYPE 96F) "FISHBED-J"

The MiG-21MF was a "second generation" aircraft with a PFMA-type tail and dorsal fairing (to improve drag characteristics), improved RP-22S "Jay Bird" radar and uprated tyres and brakes which, like the gun pod, were choices influenced by the Indian Air Force's purchase of the similar MiG-21M. MiG-21MFs were identified by a small F-4-style mirror above the canopy bow. "Jay Bird" still used more than 150 thermionic valves (tubes) at a time when US avionics were becoming solid state.

A welcome innovation was an angle of attack indicator, and the GSh-23L gun was built into the lower fuselage, with 200 rounds of ammunition. The jet's missile armament typically consisted of two R-3Ss and two R-3Rs, and combinations of UB-32 or UB-16 57mm rocket pods could also be carried. The R-60/R-60M "close combat" missile was another option. MiG-21MFs were produced at the Moscow and Gorkiy plants between 1970–75. From late 1972, the VPAF accepted examples of the MiG-21bis ("Fishbed-L" and "Fishbed-N"), which was a multi-role version with better low-altitude performance.

MiG-21U "MONGOL-A" AND MiG-21UM "MONGOL-B"

These were two-seat training versions of the MiG-21F-13, but the "Mongol-B" had the broader tail of later MiG-21s, an R-11F2S-300 engine and a more advanced cockpit.

F-4 PHANTOM II AND MiG-21 COMPARISON SPECIFICATIONS

	F-4D Phantom II	MiG-21MF
Powerplant	2 x General Electric J79-GE-15s, each rated at 17,000lbs maximum thrust	1 Tumanski/Gavrilov R-13-300 rated at 14,307lbs in afterburner
Dimensions		
Span	38ft 5in.	23ft 5.5in.
Length	58ft 2.4in.	51ft 8.5in. (including nose probe)
Height	16ft 6in.	13ft 5.5in.
Wing area	530 sq. ft	247 sq. ft
Weights		
Empty	28,958lb	12,882lb
Loaded (air combat)	38,781lb	19,730lb
Performance		
Max speed	1,275 knots at 40,000ft	1,204 knots at 42,640ft
Range	429 nautical miles (with two external tanks)	400 nautical miles (with two external tanks)
Climb	49,000ft per minute	21,000ft per minute
Service ceiling	59,650ft	56,740ft
Armament (air-to-air)	4 x AIM-7E Sparrow III	1 x GSh-23L gun
	4 x AIM-9E/J Sidewinder	2 x R-3S missiles
	1 x SUU-23/A gun pod	2 x R-3R missiles

A MiG-21UM "Mongol-B" of the 921st FR departs on yet another training mission in the autumn of 1972, while MiG-21MFs are readied for the next round of missions against US fighter-bombers. MiG-21MF 5121 was used by Pham Thuan to "down" a B-52D on the night of December 27, 1972. The USAF claimed that both the Stratofortresses lost that night were destroyed by SAMs.

THE STRATEGIC SITUATION

OPERATION *ROLLING THUNDER*

When 64 US Navy aircraft first bombed North Vietnamese targets on August 5, 1964 in response to alleged torpedo boat attacks on American destroyers, the communist North was already prepared for war. Nevertheless, in the wake of this initial attack, there was a rapid bolstering of radar, missile and fighter defenses as North Vietnam's communist allies poured in resources.

Most of the country's viable military targets were situated around the capital, Hanoi, and the docks at Haiphong, so the fighter airfields, guns and, eventually, surface-to-air missiles (SAMs) were focussed there too. Yet President Lyndon Johnson's policy of gradualism ruled out attacks on most of these targets until the last few months of the war. In later years he wrote that "our goals in Vietnam were limited, and so were our actions."

The Pentagon's analysis of the North Vietnamese build-up concluded that its integrated air defense system, including 65 fighters, was in place by August 1966. By the end of 1972 it conceded that:

> The North Vietnamese had what was generally conceded to be one of the best air defense systems in the world. It should have been – it was battle-tested for twice as long as any such system in history. Among its strongest features were excellent radar integration, the SA-2 missile and the MiG-21.

The expansion of VPAF bases had to be done with simple equipment and manual labour. When limited attacks on Kep and Hoa Lac bases were finally sanctioned by Washington in April 1967, aircraft were given basic protection in earth revetments, where maintenance was performed in the open with portable equipment and considerable ingenuity. Although the trees had grown back by the time this photograph was taken in 2007, this Noi Bai MiG-21 revetment shows how basic the facilities were. Forty years earlier, pairs of MiG-21s stood on five-minute alert, taxiing from the revetment area straight onto the runway, followed by a second pair three minutes later if needed. From radar detection of a US raid approaching from Thailand to interception by the MiGs would take little more than 20 minutes.

The instigation of Operation *Rolling Thunder* saw a dramatic increase in the scope of the American air offensive. During the campaign's opening strikes on March 2, 1965, five USAF fighters were lost and 1Lt Hayden Lockhart became the Air Force's first prisoner-of-war. In an attack on the Thanh Hoa bridge on April 3–4, among the seven USAF aircraft lost were two F-105s that became the first victims of the MiG-17 – three MiGs were shot down in return. On January 15, 1966, USAF pilots sighted MiG-21F-13s for the first time, the new fighter type having joined the MiG-17s at Noi Bai air base in late November 1965.

American strategists were concerned by the appearance of MiG-21s, and in December 1966 they predicted that it would achieve a 3-to-1 kill ratio advantage over the F-4 Phantom II above 20,000ft – the MiG's optimum operational environment. When it was seen that most Vietnam air engagements were occurring at lower altitudes, the strategists altered their prediction to 5-to-1 in the Phantom II's favor. In fact, F-4 crews were only able to achieve a ratio of a little over 2-to-1 against the MiG-21.

Pentagon predictions for the F-105 in similar circumstances were also wide of the mark. Its prediction of 4-to-1 to the MiG-21s was in fact more like 16-to-0, although Thunderchiefs did gun down 28 MiG-17s.

To match this increased threat, the USAF improved its radar coverage through the employment of EC-121D *College Eye* surveillance aircraft from the 552nd Airborne Early Warning & Control Wing that worked alongside US Navy *Red Crown* SPS-30 and SPS-48 radar-equipped picket ships sailing just off the coast of North Vietnam.

921st FR MiG-21F-13s line-up at Noi Bai (Phuc Yen) in the mid-1960s. At this early stage of the MiG-21's VPAF career, it was known that such a tempting target was out of bounds to American bombers. The third aircraft in the row is a MiG-21U "Mongol-A." Known in the USSR as the "sparka" or "twin," this two-seat trainer carried more fuel than the single-seat version.

College Eye, assigned to the Tactical Air Control Centre at Monkey Mountain, near the South Vietnamese air base at Da Nang, maintained daily EC-121D orbits over Laos and two over the Gulf of Tonkin from October 13, 1966.

To achieve the best radar performance, the Tonkin "Alpha" orbit aircraft had to fly below 500ft – and sometimes as low as 50ft – over the sea. The sweltering conditions inside the aircraft, which were packed with hot-running, valve-operated electronic equipment, but with little in the way of air-conditioning, meant that a flight surgeon had to be carried to monitor the health of the onboard controllers. Radar sites were later established at Nakhon Phanom, near the Laotian border with Thailand, and (briefly) at Site 85 in the Laotian mountains in an attempt to "see into" North Vietnam.

These over-complex and security-ridden systems were seldom as useful to USAF pilots as the North Vietnamese radar coverage was to their counterparts flying MiG fighters. Indeed, the VPAF was totally reliant on its efficient Ground Control Intercept (GCI) network when it came to engaging American fighter-bombers and their escorts. The USAF's 1974 *Red Baron III* report described this system as being run by a, "skilled, highly experienced, well-organised team."

The role of the controller was as critical as that of the MiG pilot, and more important than the contribution of the other pilot (or pilots) in his flight. As the report explained, unlike American fighter crews, "North Vietnamese aircrew did not depend on other members of the flight for mutual support".

Although most of the MiG-21 variants used by the VPAF could carry a gun, it was only used for one confirmed kill in Vietnam – two F-105Ds were hit by cannon fire from MiG-21s on April 28, 1967 and one crashed, killing the pilot. For the rest of their successful stabbing attacks, the "Atoll" missile was the preferred weapon, even though it meant that the attack had to be made from almost directly behind the target aircraft.

In those circumstances, effective ground control was vital to position the MiG for its one-chance attack, even after the introduction of the MiG-21PF series (and later), which came fitted with proper radar equipment. However, the possibility of a gun attack remained, and to dispel any doubts in combat, all Phantom II crews were told to assume that all MiGs had cannon.

VPAF fighter pilots were tasked with point defense of a limited area, mainly around the country's industrial and logistical areas – the port of Haiphong and the capital, Hanoi. GCI radar coverage extended up to 150 miles beyond the country's borders, enabling controllers to position MiGs well in advance of incoming American attacks at or above 15,000ft. Their Soviet-style GCI, when fully developed, required pilots to follow exact instructions throughout their interceptions, coordinated in a "layered" system of anti-aircraft artillery (AAA) guns, fighters and SA-2 (Soviet S-75 "Dvina") SAMs. The latter claimed their first victim (a 47th TFS F-4C) on July 24, 1965.

MiG-17s (and, in due course, MiG-19s) were used to intercept at medium and low altitude, where their maneuvrability and gun armament gave them an advantage in close, turning fights. Tactics developed for the MiG-21 optimized its supersonic performance at high altitude, where pairs of jets could be positioned by GCI to make slashing missile attacks from behind US strike formations. The fighters would then make their escape at high speed before MiGCAP F-4s could prevent American losses.

For the Vietnamese, Head Ground Controller Le Thanh Chon became one of the most skilful and intuitive operators. Later in the war, the US Navy *Red Crown* controller Senior Chief Radarman Larry Nowell gained fame for guiding Phantom II pilots to six MiG kills.

The North Vietnamese GCI task was made easier because US strike aircraft tended to use the same routes and arrival times. This policy persisted throughout the war, and cost the USAF several B-52s during the *Linebacker* raids because the defenders knew exactly where to salvo their SAMs and AAA for the maximum destructive effect. MiG-21 pilots, on the other hand, tried to avoid being predictable when they had the chance to use their own initiative. This sometimes happened when GCI gave them incorrect information, or was late in passing on warnings or direction changes.

While MiG-21 pilots made their brief interceptions over familiar, well-defended terrain, USAF Phantom II crews had to make long, complex flights in close and relatively slow formations from bases in South Vietnam and Thailand. They depended upon two or more air refuellings from tankers en route orbiting over Laos and South Vietnam, and on support from airborne radar, reconnaissance and rescue units.

Most MiGCAP flights were provided by the 8th TFW at Ubon RTAFB, in Thailand, after December 8, 1965. The second of its twelve wartime commanders, World War II ace Col Robin Olds, led the wing through some of its heaviest *Rolling*

A MiG-21PFM, showing its broader vertical fin which virtually cured the problems of engine flame-out due to lack of stability and "yawing" at high speed – a problem already solved in the USAF's early Century Series fighters like the F-100 by similar means. The pointed fairing above the jet-pipe housed a PT-21UK braking parachute, and the antenna projecting from the spine behind the upper fuel tank fairing was for the R-802V VHF radio.

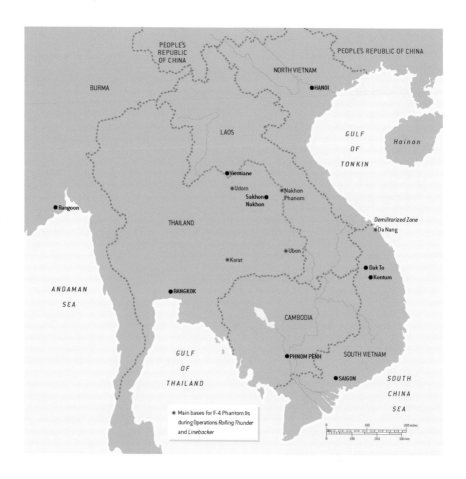

Thunder fighting from September 1966 to September 1967. During this period the 8th scored 18 MiG kills for the loss of three F-4Cs, the first of which, on October 5, 1966, saw a Phantom II downed by an "Atoll" fired from a MiG-21. This was the first success credited to the R-3S missile in VPAF service, although no MiG-21 pilots actually claimed any kills on the 5th.

Olds' legacy of aggressive tactics and leadership helped the 8th TFW to score another 14 MiG kills in the five months following his departure.

At the end of 1965, USAF air power in South-east Asia comprised 237 aircraft in Thailand and 480 at bases in South Vietnam. Of these, 108 were F-4Cs. At Cam Ranh Bay, in South Vietnam, the four-squadron 12th TFW concentrated on attacking targets inside South Vietnam. Also based in South Vietnam, at Da Nang, the 366th TFW "Gunfighters" flew F-4Cs and shared MiGCAP duties with the 8th TFW over the north towards the end of *Rolling Thunder*. The wing downed 17 MiGs from November 1966 onwards. At Korat RTAFB, in Thailand, the 388th TFW converted to the F-4E Phantom II when its handful of surviving F-105s were withdrawn in 1969. The wing duly added another seven MiG-21s and three MiG-19s to the Phantom II's "scoreboard" in *Linebacker* operations in 1972.

For the opposition, the MiG-21 force comprised only 16 aircraft at the end of 1966, but it increased steadily as MiG-21s replaced MiG-17s. The VPAF's force

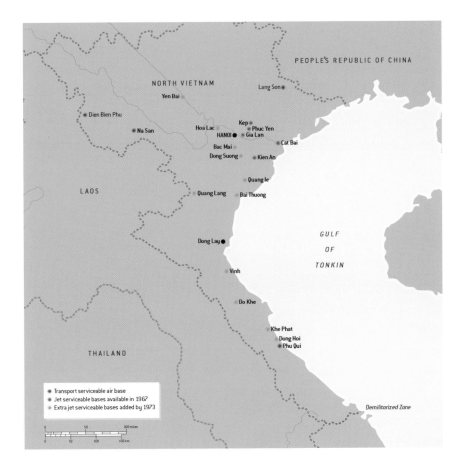

Noi Bai (Phuc Yen) was the first MiG-21 base, later joined by Kep and Gia Lam. After *Rolling Thunder*, new forward bases were established nearer the demilitarized zone and the Laotian border for attempts at B-52 interception. Dong Suong, Quang Lang and Yen Bai were the best equipped of these bases.

strength eventually peaked at around 45 serviceable aircraft in 1972. Deliveries of MiGs of all types from China and the USSR appear to have averaged about 40 per year throughout the war.

Seventh Air Force Commander Gen William "Spike" Momyer announced on August 16, 1967 that "We have driven the MiGs out of the sky for all practical purposes. The MiGs are no longer a threat." His judgement reflected the heavy losses suffered by the MiG force that summer, but it was very premature. He attributed the low success rate against MiGs at other times to "political constraints." Certainly, many F-4 pilots felt that destroying the MiGs in Haiphong docks before they could be assembled and flown would have been more logical than waiting to be jumped by them in combat!

OPERATION *LINEBACKER*

Following the ending of the US bombing halt that had lasted from April 1968 through to January 1972, US aircraft started mounting renewed attacks on North Vietnam to try and break its support for increasing Viet Cong activity in the south. In 1988,

President Johnson's successor, Richard Nixon, described the "bombing halt" as his greatest mistake, saying "We would have ended the war in 1969, rather than 1973." His Operation *Linebacker* attacks in 1972 could have been used to destroy the limited numbers of strategic military and industrial targets in North Vietnam much earlier, but fear of bringing the USSR and China directly into the war had deterred Washington.

These same fears initially prevented attacks on VPAF MiG airfields and radar installations, where Soviet technical advisors were thought to be working. By 1972, Russian and Chinese political support for the North Vietnamese regime had declined, and Nixon could use air power with fewer constraints to extricate the USA from the conflict, while at the same time giving overt support to South Vietnam's President Nguyen Van Thieu as aggression from the North increased.

US troops had been substantially withdrawn from the area after *Rolling Thunder* had ended, and renewed hostilities depended heavily upon air power. As part of the build-up, Phantom IIs returned to Thailand with the arrival of the 432nd Tactical Reconnaissance Wing (TRW) at Udorn. This base duly hosted nine F-4D/E squadrons and detachments at various times up to June 1975, when military activity in Laos and Cambodia was still occurring. The 388th TFW's F-4Es at Korat RTAFB also remained until war's end. At Da Nang, the 366th TFW had converted to F-4Es in 1969 and transferred to Takhli RTAFB in June 1972, and it subsequently deployed several squadrons to Udorn's 432nd TRW.

During *Rolling Thunder*, USAF fighter wings usually comprised two or three squadrons, each of 18 aircraft, several of which would be undergoing maintenance at any time. During 1972, squadron size increased to 24 Phantom IIs and 30 two-man crews, including several on their second or third tours. Squadrons were divided into

The effectiveness of the iconic MiG-21 in its designated role as an interceptor in Soviet and North Vietnamese service depended upon effective guidance from ground controllers using radar like the mobile P-35 "Bar Lock," with its 300km range, seen in the background of this photograph. The MiG-21PFM parked in front of the radar was flown by ace Nguyen Tien Sam, who claimed six kills (all USAF F-4s) with the 927th FR "Lam Son." Seen here on display in Hanoi, it is still equipped with supersonic drop tank and two "Atolls" – a typical combat fit.

flights of four (denoted by a call sign in battle). Each flight had two elements of two aircraft (sometimes using a colour identifier), each led by an experienced pilot, with a "new guy" wingman. The flight leader was usually the most experienced flyer, but not necessarily the most senior in rank (also true of MiG-21 pilots).

Their main purpose as fighters was to escort strike flights of bombers, *Iron Hand* radar attackers, tankers or reconnaissance aircraft, in addition to performing the staple duty of ground attack. The F-4 wings usually designated one squadron as its MiGCAP provider, and the 555th TFS carried out this duty more than any other unit. During *Linebacker*, additional duties included dropping chaff canisters to "blind" radars during B-52 attacks.

MiG-21s also operated in four-aircraft flights, but usually attacked as pairs or threes. Two or three flights comprised a squadron (about eight MiGs), and a fighter regiment, commanded by a captain ("thuong ui") or major ("thieu ta"), included two or three squadrons. Three regiments made up an air division, commanded by a colonel ("thuong ta") or major general ("thieu tuong"). A second MiG-21 unit, the 927th FR "Lam Son" was formed on February 3, 1972 and equipped with the MiG-21PFM. The 921st FR, led by ace Nguyen Hong Nhi, had by then already converted onto the advanced MiG-21MF.

Operational MiG-21 numbers rarely exceeded 45 aircraft during the war due to heavy losses, particularly of pilots. In contrast to the secure, well-equipped USAF bases, VPAF airfields came under frequent air attack after April 1967, forcing the fighters to operate from covert Chinese bases for long periods, thus severely disrupting maintenance and training.

During *Linebacker II*, a shortage of pilots meant that many new MiG-21s were stored in caves, where they were often rendered useless through corrosion. The lack of skilled Russian or Chinese technicians reduced operational readiness to less than 30

The pilot and groundcrew of MiG-21PFM 5006 line up for inspection in 1972 during a visit by the Prime Minister of Hungary. Training proficient groundcrew was as vital as the provision of qualified pilots. Chinese advisors trained and assisted technicians working on Chinese-built Shenyang J-5 (MiG-17) and J-6 (MiG-19) aircraft, and around 30 Russian advisors were kept busy on the MiG-21s at Noi Bai, Kep and Gia Lam.

TAC's basic "fluid four" fighter formation dated back to World War II, and it proved to be too inflexible for use in Vietnam. The leading aircraft was the designated "shooter," while the other three crews concentrated on protecting him. The formation would spread out when chasing a MiG, making the number four aircraft (at the extreme right in this diagram) more vulnerable.

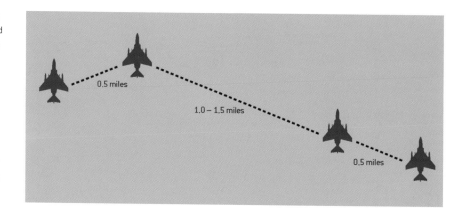

The standard MiG-21 formation was known as "hi-lo singles," a variation on the "hi-lo pairs" four-aircraft formation used by MiG-17s. Often, a third MiG-21 would "trail" two miles behind the pair, and he would actually be the main "shooter."

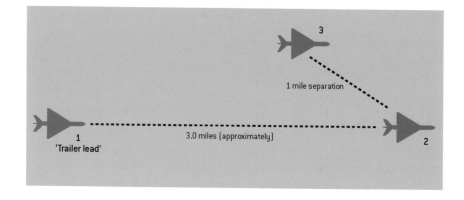

per cent at times. Frequent attacks on their airfields also forced the MiGs that remained in North Vietnam to disperse, often being airlifted under huge Mi-6 helicopters, based at Gia Lam, to smaller, rough fields, where they could make rocket-assisted take-offs and then be hidden in caves or structures such as farm buildings upon their return.

The 308th TFS managed to paint a sharksmouth (echoed in miniature on its underwing tanks) on F-4E 67-0239 at Udorn RTAFB during its assignment to the 432nd TRW in 1972. However, the markings soon had to be removed on the express orders of the wing commander. The aircraft is seen here resplendent in its unique markings, configured for a MiGCAP "up north" during *Linebacker*.

THE COMBATANTS

The fighter pilots from the two opposing air forces that fought each other over North Vietnam came from very different military traditions. USAF pilots' training and tactics were rooted in the experience of World War II and the Korean War in an air force that traced its origins back to the US Army's use of observation balloons in 1840.

A number of pilots brought direct experience of previous conflicts to the F-4 community, including the legendary Col Robin Olds. A member of the 1943 West Point class, he had destroyed 13 German aircraft flying P-38 Lightnings and P-51 Mustangs during World War II. In 1966, when he took over the 8th TFW at Ubon RTAFB, his Deputy Commander, Col Daniel "Chappie" James, had also flown Mustangs against the Luftwaffe. The Vice-Wing Commander, Col Vermont Garrison, had shot down 7.333 German aircraft flying Thunderbolts and Mustangs during World War II and ten MiG-15s in Korea in 1953.

Garrison was just one of dozens of USAF pilots to have entered the world's first jet-versus-jet conflict over North Korea with a solid grounding in gunnery and dogfighting from World War II to draw on, resulting in American fighters pilots (predominantly flying F-86 Sabres) claiming 560 kills and attaining a 7-to-1 kill-to-loss ratio. Some 42 USAF pilots became aces in the conflict, and as late as 1972 there were still a few "old head" Korean War-period aviators serving in the frontline. Indeed, the crew of one of the May 1972 MiG killer F-4Ds, Lt Cols Wayne Frye and Jim Cooney, had a combined age of 85, but by then they were exceptions.

To supply the expanding war requirements, many pilots were much younger and came from Replacement Training Units (RTUs). The "old heads'" experience was informally available at squadron level, but air-to-air skills were inadequately covered in F-4 training at George and McDill AFBs. USAF policy of rotating crews after 100 missions (or a year in South Vietnam) meant many experienced F-4 flyers were

A 433rd TFS/8th TFW crew dismount from their F-4C at Ubon RTAFB during Operation *Bolo* in January 1967. This squadron claimed no fewer than six MiG-21s destroyed between January 2, 1967 and February 6, 1968.

moved to other "career enhancing" posts early in the war.

From 1967 onwards, RTUs were filling the increasing gaps by rapidly processing aircrew transferred from over-staffed Strategic Air Command (SAC) bomber squadrons or transport units on the assumption that any USAF pilot could fly any aircraft type, given basic conversion training. Thereby, many pilots who did not qualify for fighter slots in their initial training were put into fighters, although in reality they were still unsuitable for fast jet jobs. This first became obvious in combat to the disadvantage of their units. The constant changeover of personnel also weakened squadron integrity. US Navy F-4 squadrons, on the other hand, stayed together for a whole combat tour that typically lasted four to six months, giving greater cohesion.

Although little more than ten years had passed since the ending of the Korean War, air warfare had changed so much that dogfighting skills had been virtually phased out of USAF training. Fighters had become missile-armed interceptors of bombers, or strike-fighters for high-speed tactical nuclear attack. Fighter design emphasis was on speed, altitude and weapons load, rather than close-combat, air-to-air capability and maneuvrability using guns. SAC dominated the USAF budget with its big bomber mentality, and Gen William Momyer had to maintain Tactical Air Command's purpose by selecting aircraft with nuclear attack capability.

Fighter-versus-fighter training with costly jets like the F-4 was considered unnecessary and dangerous – many pilots had been lost in training for Korea at Nellis AFB in the early 1950s. Crews were discouraged or even banned from air combat practice. Informal air combat maneuvering (ACM) against similar jets happened, but it provided no realistic preparation for facing the very different performances and tactics of Soviet-designed jets, and their pilots. F-4 crews at Ubon RTAFB were unusually fortunate in having Royal Australian Air Force CA-27 Sabre Mk 32s sharing their base, and they offered them some realistic MiG-17 simulation.

A limited program called *Feather Duster* was run in 1965 when it was realised that US pilots would face MiGs in Vietnam, and it graphically showed that F-4 and F-105 crews would be in real trouble if they engaged them at close quarters. The study questioned the USAF's Luftwaffe-derived fighting wing combat formation in which a flight leader was the "shooter" and the other three fighters flew in close formation with him, effectively protecting his tail, but usually being denied kill opportunities themselves.

555th TFS/432nd TRW crew Capt Bryan Tibbett (left) and 1Lt William "Bud" Hargrove (center) talk tactics with US Navy exchange pilot Lt Cdr Mike Ettel of the 58th TFS/432nd TRW at Udorn RTAFB in September 1972. Tibbett and Hargrove were credited with two MiG-21s destroyed in September 1972, while Ettel (crewed with US Marine Corps exchange pilot Capt Larry Richard) had claimed his "Fishbed" kill a month earlier.

Nevertheless, this tactic was sustained throughout the war, and supported by the USAF's tactics-shaping Fighter Weapons School, rather than accepting the more effective US Navy use of mutually-supportive pairs of fighters. As MiG killer Steve Wayne observed, "A lack of sufficient training in air-to-air combat and some outmoded World War II tactics such as the fighting wing certainly hampered the F-4, which was really an extremely versatile multi-role fighter".

Terry Talley, also a MiG killer, added that in 1967 some relief was provided as "a lot of our pilots came from USAFE, where they did have some experience with guns" in their previous F-100 and F-105 units. Some revision of training had to be introduced when it was seen that pilots would have to contend with the missile-firing MiG-21 as well as the guns-only, short-range threat of the MiG-17.

In F-4 training, some 94 per cent of the syllabus was devoted to air-to-ground tactics. Indeed, the vast majority of USAF Phantom II pilots would earn their additional $65 a month combat pay by dropping bombs on jungle targets of dubious value and never seeing a MiG-21. In many cases, they would have been unprepared to face a VPAF fighter because of their lack of training in maneuvring combat. Brig Gen (then Col) Robin Olds disagreed profoundly with this attitude. He told the author:

Every fighter pilot should be able to fly his aircraft to the very limits of both his and his aircraft's abilities. Very seldom do the two abilities match. It is the competent pilot who recognises his own limitations vis-a-vis those of his aircraft. I pushed my crews to the limits of the least competent man in the formation. The difference between men was very slight, but worth a life in the heat of combat.

In stark contrast, the VPAF began with 30 trainees and two World War II-vintage trainers (one of which was a British Tiger Moth biplane) in 1949. In 1956,

30 students began fighter training in MiG-15s. Airfield construction commenced in 1958, beginning at Yen Bai (operational in August 1964), and an Air Force training school was established in 1959 with a few Yak-18s and MiG-15s. Fifty pilots started MiG-17 conversion training in the USSR in 1960, with 30 others receiving instruction in China on 40 MiG-17 and MiG-15UTI jets donated by Russia in 1962.

The VPAF's first fighter regiment, the 921st "Sao Dao", was established at Mong Tu, in China, on 3 February 1964 – it soon moved to Noi Bai, north of Hanoi. After a brief preparation, its inexperienced pilots were sent into combat to oppose American crews just over a year later.

Unlike their US counterparts, surviving VPAF pilots fought right through the war, rather than undertaking fixed tours of duty. The first cadre of pilots was selected from well-educated serving army or navy officers who had strong nationalistic motivation and preferably some experience of fighting the French in the conflict that ended at Dien Bien Phu in 1954. With recruits of such a high caliber, the VPAF was far from being the "peasant" air corps that some Americans expected, although different economic circumstances meant that most Vietnamese pilots flew a fast jet before they drove a car! The ideological requirements were so demanding that many very promising students were rejected because they could not demonstrate to their political mentors sufficient loyalty to Vietnamese nationalism.

Very strict physical standards were also required. MiG fighters lacked the augmented controls of American jets, so considerable strength was needed when it came to performing maneuvers, particularly at high speeds. The slightly built Vietnamese found this aspect of aerial combat difficult to get to grips with.

Recruits needed a completed secondary education, and most students learned enough Russian to follow basic instructions and understand the rudiments of the MiG manuals. Translators were always in demand, however. Teaching was by "rote," and everything had to be done strictly by the book. There was absolutely no room for a "wild blue yonder" fighter pilot mentality, although some pilots tended to forget this when they first went into combat.

VPAF aircrew were always encouraged to study any published material on the Luftwaffe and other fighter doctrines, as were F-4 crews. Historical defensive actions such as the Battle of Britain had particular significance for the Vietnamese. Their motivation in defending their home soil was strong, and inspired courage that made up for small numbers. Fighting over friendly territory obviously gave VPAF pilots great advantages that were denied to their USAF brethren, although a few communist aviators who ejected were shot by mistake nevertheless.

MiG-21 training in the USSR was conducted on L-29 and two-seat MiG-21U "Mongol" aircraft, with continuation training being undertaken in North Vietnam. Often, VPAF pilots would find themselves learning alongside students from other Communist bloc air forces. Several Cuban advisors also worked with the VPAF on MiG tactics pre-war.

Suitable training aircraft were scarce in North Vietnam throughout the war, and this meant that most instructional flying occurred abroad. In the early years of the VPAF, MiG pilots took up to five years to complete their conversion while flying with Chinese instructors at bases near Beijing.

Throughout the war, there were reports that US pilots had seen Russian aviators flying combat missions, but these accounts were strenuously denied by the North Vietnamese. It is likely that Vietnamese national pride would have prevented Russians from acting in anything other than an advisory role.

MiG-21F-13s first appeared with the 921st FR (the unit with the most MiG-17 experience), and the regiment commenced operational flying with the jet in January 1966. The 921st, commanded by Tran Hinh, took on another 13 pilots six months

Pham Thanh Ngan (right), who was one of the top VPAF aces with eight kills to his credit, describes one of his dogfights to Nguyen Van Coc. The latter flew more than 550 wartime missions – some pilots logged over 600.

Tran Hanh (left), CO of the 921st FR, and one of the first VPAF pilots to transition from the MiG-17 to the MiG-21, briefs his pilots at Noi Bai in 1966. All of them are wearing the tight-fitting green high-altitude flying suits synonymous with "Fishbed" operations in the early war years. The pilots' personal equipment is completed by a bulky GS-4 helmet — a far cry from the SL-60 leather helmet that they would have worn when flying the MiG-15UTI and JJ-5 during conversion training. Two MiG-21PF "Fishbed-Ds" of the 921st can be seen parked in the background.

later, and by the end of 1966 the first MiG-21 pilot to be trained inside North Vietnam, Dong Van De, had shot down an F-105D. Accompanying Van De on that mission was Nguyen Van Coc, who was already seen as being one of the most capable pilots in the squadron.

With such small numbers of pilots and aircraft, losses were acutely felt. Sometimes, a whole squadron of eight MiGs could be lost in a few days. VPAF pilots inevitably thought that their more numerous rivals had superior training and equipment. Typically facing odds of 6-to-1 against them, Vietnamese pilots had to minimize their exposure to American firepower.

However, MiG pilots could devote all their skills and training to intercepting the Americans under increasingly effective ground control. Their short missions enabled each pilot to fly three or four interceptions daily at the height of the air war, normally facing four big USAF and US Navy strike packages each day. This resulted in pilots accruing some enormous mission totals – Nguyen Nhat Chieu, for example, claimed six kills during the course of 600 missions.

MiG-21 pilots gave their adversaries an impression of hesitancy and inexperience during *Rolling Thunder*, but by the time *Linebacker* operations commenced in 1972, a number of US pilots commented on how they envied their VPAF opponents their speedy and maneuvrable steeds, and respected the flying skills they had mastered with such a small force. A well-controlled pair of MiG-21s, coordinated with SAMs and MiG-17s operating at lower altitudes, could severely disrupt a strike formation by destroying two or three aircraft in a single supersonic pass, before escaping the MiGCAP F-4s and running for sanctuary in China.

Many VPAF pilots earned the respect of their USAF opponents. MiG-killer Col John Madden told the author:

They were formidable opponents. They used an awful lot of ruses and deceptions. It was clear that they were very disciplined, thinking things through carefully. They loved to set traps. It was just through the sheer numbers of aircraft we put up that we were able to overpower them.

The four-year "bombing pause" had allowed the VPAF to increase its MiG-21 force from 38 to 94 jets, with all pilots having converted to the MiG-21PFM or the advanced MiG-21MF by the end of 1971. Airfield runways had also been extended and dispersal areas suitably "hardened" to better withstand air attacks, although most MiG bases were badly damaged by bombing raids during *Linebacker I*, launched in May 1972. Forward bases were established within an expanded GCI network to assist with the MiG pilots' ultimate goal – the downing of a B-52.

In an effort to achieve the latter, 18 pilots received night interception training. New tactics were also devised that saw MiG-21s attacking the bombers in zoom-climbs from radar-dodging low altitudes. Several such attacks were defeated by B-52 crews launching flares that deflected well-aimed "Atolls". Phantom IIs were also put on five-minute alert at Da Nang and Udorn, with crews instructed to prevent the loss of a B-52 to a MiG-21. VPAF pilot Dinh Ton was specially trained as a B-52 slayer, although Vu Dinh Rang was the first to be credited with damaging one on November 20, 1971.

The topic for instruction for these 927th FR pilots seems to be "how fighter pilots use their hands to re-enact combat successes"! By the time this photograph was taken in 1972, leather flying jackets and ZS-3 helmets had long since replaced the cumbersome G-suits and bulky GS-4 helmets that had initially been issued to pilots when the MiG-21s arrived in North Vietnam in late 1965.

NGUYEN VAN COC

Born in the Viet Yen District, north of Hanoi, in 1942, Nguyen Van Coc was the son of a Viet Minh resistance leader who was assassinated by the occupying French forces. His mother had to spirit her son away to Thai Nguyen, near to Chu air base, where the boy became fascinated with aircraft. While in his senior year at Ngo Si Lien school in Bac Giang, Van Coc took basic recruitment tests for the air force and was accepted in 1961. He and 120 other trainees were subsequently sent to Russia for four years, training at Batajsk and Krasnodov. Only 17 were eventually selected for MiG-17 training, and just seven students, including Van Coc, managed to attain the grade of pilot.

Returning to Noi Bai (Phuc Yen) in a MiG-17 with the 921st FR, he was soon sent back to the USSR with 13 other pilots to undertake conversion training onto the MiG-21. Rejoining his unit (by now equipped with MiG-21s) at Noi Bai in June 1966, Van Coc passed on his knowledge to a follow-on batch of pilots who were trained in North Vietnam using MiG-15UTIs because there were no two-seat MiG-21Us then available.

Van Coc began operational flying in December 1966, and although shot down during Operation *Bolo*, he enjoyed success on April 30, 1967 when flying as wingman to future ace Nguyen Ngoc Do. Moments before Van Coc's engagement, an F-105F from the 355th TFW had been shot down by squadronmate Le Trong Huyen. Minutes later, Ngoc Do and Van Coc fired their "Atolls" at two F-105Ds from the same wing, downing both jets. A third Thunderchief, flown by Maj Al Lenski, was also hit by an air-to-air missile, but the pilot managed to nurse his badly damaged Thunderchief back to Udorn.

Flying as wingman became something of a Van Coc trademark, and most of his kills were made from that position. It yielded an element of surprise in that the enemy would expect the formation leader to be the shooter. This technique was incorporated into the VPAF's training, thus proving that some flexibility was allowed for good individual input.

Nguyen Van Coc perfected his technique of approaching the enemy cautiously and firing a missile at maximum range, following up with a second shot if

necessary, and then diving for safety. "Atolls" were used for all nine of his kills. A 555th TFS F-4D was his second victim on August 23, 1967 – a day when "Triple Nickel" lost four F-4Ds, two to MiG-21s. Two more confirmed F-105Ds followed, with a third remaining unconfirmed. An unusual kill, and one which Van Coc rightly regarded as a special personal trophy, was the 509th FIS F-102A of 1Lt Wallace Wiggins that he destroyed on February 3, 1968. This was destined to be the only Delta Dagger lost by the USAF in combat.

Of Van Coc's nine claims, all but two coincide with US records, including a Firebee drone that the VPAF counted as a kill, making him the ranking ace of the Vietnam War on either side.

In 1969, 27-year-old Van Coc was singled out for particular praise by the Vietnamese President, Ho Chi Minh, and awarded a Huy Hieu ("Uncle Ho") medal for each of his kills. He withdrew from combat after *Rolling Thunder* to concentrate on training future MiG-21 pilots. Van Coc eventually became Commander of the Vietnamese National Air Forces, before retiring in 2002 as Chief Inspector of the Ministry of Defense following a prolonged period of ill health.

ROBIN OLDS

The son of a World War I fighter pilot who became a USAAC major general, Robin Olds was born in Honolulu, Hawaii, in July 1922. In the year of Nguyen Van Coc's birth, Olds was selected as an All American tackle, and he graduated from the US Military Academy at West Point in June 1943.

Having made his first flight in his father's biplane at the age of eight, it was unsurprising that Olds immediately sought the chance to participate in "Hitler's War." He sailed to England with the 479th FG in May 1944, and subsequently saw combat in the P-38J Lightning. "Making ace" in the latter aircraft on August 25, Olds switched to the P-51 Mustang the following month, and by war's end his score stood at 13 aerial and 11 strafing victories.

Post-war, Olds was an early convert to jets, flying the P-80 Shooting Star. An RAF exchange tour saw him become the first USAF exchange officer to command a British fighter unit when he was made CO of Meteor F 4-equipped No. 1 Sqn at Tangmere, in West Sussex, in October 1948. Olds was accurately described by the unit's historian as being "one of the dominant personalities in the squadron."

It was his feisty character and intolerance of what he saw as inappropriate USAF policies that kept Olds from attaining squadron command in the Korean War, and he reluctantly sat out that conflict with staff jobs and as CO of the 71st FIS, assigned to Air Defense Command in the USA. His return to Europe as wing leader of the F-86-equipped 86th FIW took him to Landstuhl AB, in Germany, after which further Pentagon and National War College assignments followed. Olds was then made CO of the 81st TFW, equipped with F-101 Voodoos, at RAF Bentwaters until 1965. His command was withdrawn after Third Air Force HQ objected to his unofficial aerobatic display team.

Despite his rather individualistic attitude to authority, no selection panel could ignore the unstinting devotion that Olds inspired in any unit he commanded, and thus 22 years after his last World War II dogfight, he found himself in charge of the F-4C-equipped 8th TFW at Ubon RTAFB. He quickly revived fighter skills within the wing that had been all but lost in a decade of training that was inappropriate for the war.

Olds' first of four MiG kills came during Operation *Bolo* (his own concept) on January 2, 1967, followed by a second on May 4. Having claimed two MiG-21s, he then downed a pair of MiG-17s on May 20. Olds led by example, flying 105 of his 152 Southeast Asia missions over North Vietnam, and allegedly shunning several other MiG-kill opportunities in case he was relieved of command and sent on a publicity tour as the first USAF Vietnam ace!

Olds vocal support for conventional warfare skills in a nuclear-war dominated Air Force remained unpopular with the "senior management," so he was removed from the war zone after completing his tour and made Commandant of Cadets at the USAF Academy for three years, and then Director of Aerospace Safety. This took him to Thailand during *Linebacker II*, after which he presented his assessment of the fighter pilots' combat readiness. It said, "They couldn't fight their way out of a wet paper bag." Faced with Olds' evidence, senior officers in the USAF accepted his verdict and set about getting air combat training taken more seriously.

Robin Olds retired in June 1973 and began work on his autobiography, which, sadly, remained unfinished at the time of his death on June 14, 2007.

COMBAT

Following the first MiG-17 kills by 45th TFS F-4Cs on July 10, 1965, the first MiG-21 claims were made on April 26, 1966 by the 480th TFS. An earlier opportunity was missed when a pilot was unable to take advantage of a perfect shot at a MiG-21 because his groundcrew had forgotten to connect the F-4C's AIM-7 launch ejection devices – and then all its AIM-9s failed too! In the same engagement two MiG-21 pilots could not launch their R-3Ss either because they could not train the narrow beam of their SRD-5M range-finding radars onto the F-4s.

MiG-21 pilots fired 14 "Atolls" during April–May 1966 without success at a time when they were mainly flying practice interceptions or patrols near Hanoi. Reading the small radar indicator panel while following a maneuvring target, then switching to the ASP-5ND optical gunsight was an exercise in coordination that defeated the inexperienced VPAF flyers at that stage.

The first confirmed "Atoll" success for the MiG-21 did not come until October 5, 1966, when an F-4C was shot down, followed on December 14, 1966 by an F-105D. Guided weapon problems were a persistent handicap for both the USAF and VPAF, and aviators on both sides wanted guns in their fighters. The MiG-21 pilots got theirs first.

The April 26, 1966 engagement revealed many of the strengths and weaknesses on both sides. Three 480th TFS F-4Cs were escorting an EB-66 radar jamming jet, and flight leader Maj Paul Gilmore set up an orbit north of Hanoi. The Phantom II crews soon detected a pair of MiG-21s closing from almost head-on, so Gilmore sent the EB-66 away to safety and ordered his flight to jettison their drop tanks. Turning hard left and diving in afterburner, Gilmore and his "GIB" ("guy in back"), 1Lt W. T. Smith, then climbed behind the MiGs that were 18,000ft above them.

Although the MiG-21s had been vectored correctly towards the EB-66, their pilots had not noticed Gilmore's element, probably due to their restricted cockpit view. With a "blind spot" extending aft from the leading edge of the wing, and very little downward visibility, a MiG pilot could easily miss a pair of smoky Phantom IIs. F-4 back-seaters had a fairly crude solution to even worse rearward vision. In his report following his May 20, 1967 double MiG-killing mission, Col Olds (who was flying his 56th F-4 combat sortie) noted, "By using the (instrument panel) glare-shield as a hand-hold, and keeping his shoulder harness lock open, the back-seater can pull himself out of his seat and see well towards the six o'clock position."

This obviously was not possible in a single-seat jet, and on April 26 one MiG-21 turned away, leaving his wingman exposed. Gilmore and his wingman passed unnoticed by the second fighter as they accelerated near-vertically to attack.

MiG killer Ralph Wetterhahn commented on another benefit from the F-4's power when the odds favored the enemy. "The only real advantage we had was to accelerate out of a fight. I'd trade that for performance any day."

On this occasion, Maj Gilmore used that power to quickly enter missile range, and he achieved several boresight radar lock-ons. With his jet already inside optimum AIM-7 range, however, Gilmore fired an AIM-9B instead just as the MiG-21 turned slowly, trying to spot them. Gilmore pulled his fighter away to gain separation, and thereby did not see his missile pass close enough to the MiG for its pilot to eject.

Returning for a second shot (that missed) Gilmore, an "old head" with 12 years in fighters, felt "quite disgusted. Then I got my sights on him and fired a third AIM-9B. I observed the missile go directly up his tailpipe and explode his tail". Radio problems had prevented Gilmore's wingman from telling him that his first missile had indeed given the USAF its premier MiG-21 kill, and since he was banking away from the enemy fighter he did not see the impact himself.

As previously mentioned, radio communications were a bugbear for F-4 crews throughout the war. In his end-of-tour report, MiG-killing ace Capt Steve Ritchie described the fighter's radio as "the single most important piece of equipment, and radio failure is unacceptably high."

The 555th TFS's 19 MiG kills during *Rolling Thunder*, followed by 20 more in 1972, earned the unit a reputation for being the "largest distributor of MiG parts in Southeast Asia." Here, "Triple Nickel" MiG killers enjoy a drink at the Udorn O'Club in July 1972. They are, in the back row, from left to right, Lt Cols Wayne Frye and Jim Cooney, Capt Larry Pettit and 1Lt John Markle. In the front row, from left to right, are Capts Doug Hardgrave, Chuck DeBellevue, Steve Ritchie and Rodger Locher.

The KC-135A tanker fleet made Phantom II missions possible in Vietnam, with in-flight refuelling taking place several times on most missions over the North. Daring rescues of fuel-starved F-4s by tanker crews who ventured closer than they should have to hostile territory were also a regular occurrence. F-4C 63-7544 was lost on December 8, 1966 while serving with the 480th TFS/366th TFW when it was hit by small-arms whilst taking off from Da Nang at night.

This April 1966 encounter also showed the inexperience of the 921st FR pilots through their failure to provide mutual support for each other, even though their GCI sent the first MiG-21 back to the area and he almost obtained a firing solution on Gilmore's jet while he and his wingman were "target fixated" with the wreckage of their victim. Luckily, Gilmore noticed the MiG-21 as he pulled up, and both Phantom IIs executed a rapid defensive split (one going left and down and the other right and up).

Anticipating another kill opportunity, Gilmore rolled in behind the "Fishbed" as it climbed away in afterburner. He fired his final AIM-9B, but he was too close and it passed over the MiG's wing. This time the pilot did not eject.

Launching missiles outside their design parameters was another typical difficulty endured by both sides during the war. Of the 21 AIM-9s fired in April–May 1966, only five scored hits. Worse, the AIM-7D achieved just one kill in 16 attempts.

The final problem typified by this fight is an historical one. Inconsistencies in claims and counter-claims in the two sides' records have often obscured the real results of these clashes over the past 40 years. VPAF documents do not list a MiG-21 loss for April 26, 1966, although several crashed due to fuel starvation in the preceding weeks – these remained unrecorded by the Pentagon. VPAF pilots did not keep personal log books, unlike their American counterparts, and the creation of detailed post-mission records was sometimes overlooked by the hard-pressed Vietnamese.

In the first round of Vietnam War engagements between April 1965 and August 1966, USAF and US Navy Phantom II units had the upper hand with 16 MiGs (including three MiG-21s) downed for the loss of only one F-4C. However, VPAF pilots learned rapidly, and throughout the rest of *Rolling Thunder* MiG-17s became more confident in close combat with the Americans at medium altitude, while the small MiG-21 force devised tactics where they dived from high altitude, fired from the rear of the strike formation and fled at high speed, eluding the MiGCAP F-4s.

From September 1966 onwards, MiGs were sighted on most days in larger groups, and on several occasions MiG-21s completed their slashing dive attacks on F-105s or

F-4s undetected by their prey, or by US radar controllers. Meanwhile, MiG-17 pilots like Nguyen Van Bay (who became the first VPAF ace on September 5, 1966 – Nguyen Van Coc was the first MiG-21 ace, claiming his fifth kill on November 18, 1967) refined Luftwaffe-style head-on attacks to break up enemy attack formations. MiG-21s possibly scored their first "Atoll" kill on October 5, 1966 when 1Lt E. W. Garland (with "GIB" Capt W. R. Andrews) in F-4C 64-0702 claimed that his jet was downed by one, although no VPAF claim was made that day.

Although the cause of this Phantom II loss remains open to conjecture, what is certain is that the increased supply of Soviet SAMs from late 1966 onwards was causing alarming American losses. MiG-21 pilots were also learning to make better use of their missiles too, and their GCI controllers had by now devised rigid, but effective, ways to guide aircraft into favorable high-altitude attack positions. Climbing attacks into the rear blind spot of US fighter-bombers were also producing results.

And while the VPAF began to get its act together, American missiles continued to behave erratically. When two MiG-21s swooped in behind an EB-66 on November 5, 1966, Maj R. E. "Friar" Tuck's flight of four F-4Cs quickly fell in astern of the intruders for what should have been two easy kills. A third MiG then appeared behind Tuck's "Opal 1" F-4C, and 1Lts Joe Latham and Klaus Klause in "Opal 2" went after it, firing an AIM-9B. "The missile came off the rail, jinked and exploded on him," Klaus Klause told the author. "The MiG looked as if it had blown up and been punched over. We broke back left and almost ran the pilot over in his 'chute."

Meanwhile, "Friar" fired all four AIM-7s at the lead MiG as it homed in on the EB-66. Three failed to guide, and Tuck (in Klause's words) "practically shoulder-charged the MiG to one side" to make it break off. He shot off his final missile as the persistent MiG pilot dived reluctantly away. "It appeared to explode just ahead of the MiG, making its engine flame out, or maybe the pilot just lost control and ejected."

Tuck's engagement illustrates the difficult "switchology" needed to fire weapons from the F-4C/D. Whilst the MiG-21 cockpit was no better laid out than the F-4's, with controls placed fairly randomly and inaccessibly, selection of missiles or guns (in the MiG-21PF/PFM) needed only two simple switch movements. When Maj Tuck realised that the motor in the first AIM-7 he had fired off had failed, he tried to switch to "heat" to achieve a target lock-on for one of his AIM-9s. However, in his haste, he turned the three-position missile switch to the wrong setting. Tuck then set up a second AIM-7, but it launched inside minimum range, and the third missile's warhead failed to arm.

"Atoll" reliability was considered to be worse than the AIM-9's even when fired from the ideal position of 1,000–1,200 yards astern of the target aircraft – twice the favored range for guns. VPAF pilots welcomed the introduction of the MiG-21PF/PFM with its gun pod and useful gun camera to record successes. Guns were reliable, and an attack from the "six o'clock low" position would usually be fatal.

Skilful GCI operators would hold back their MiGs until they heard "Bingo" fuel calls as they monitored insecure USAF radios, unleashing the "Fishbeds" in a series of stabbing attacks. The latter often targeted flak-damaged stragglers. Although engaging fleeing American aircraft allowed the MiGs to claim a number of kills, the primary objective of the VPAF was to break up attacks *before* they reached their targets, forcing the bombers to jettison their loads and defend themselves instead.

In ideal GCI conditions, a MiG-21 pilot would be radioed exact headings and instructions on how many attacks he could make, and which weapons to use. He would then be given a safe route to base, avoiding MiGCAPs. He could not go beyond the limits of his GCI area, and if anything went wrong he would usually be told to abort his attack. Phantom II and F-105 pilots would be so pre-occupied with holding "jamming pod" formation, dealing with radio communications, remembering the day's codes and call-signs and watching for SAMs and AAA that MiGs could creep in unobserved by MiGCAP F-4s or US radars.

However, the rigid Soviet GCI methods left MiG pilots with no room for initiative, and sometimes forced them to obey orders which they could see were ill-advised.

Mai Van Cuong claimed eight US aircraft destroyed with the 921st FR. As additional equipment was installed above the instrument displays in both the MiG-21 and Phantom II, the pilot's view deteriorated – F-4Es had worse forward visibility than F-4Cs, for example. This photograph shows how the addition of the RP-21M radarscope and ASP-PF-21 optical gunsight in the cockpit of the MiG-21PFM blocked the view forward.

Above all, it left them unprepared to cope with sudden changes in US tactics. Operation *Bolo* on January 2, 1967 was a good example. Faced with increasing successes by the MiG-21 force and Washington's sustained refusal (until April 24, 1967) to allow attacks on their airfields, the 8th TFW at Ubon devised a plan to remove the MiGs and, more importantly, their pilots by drawing them into battle.

When Col Robin Olds took over the 8th TFW on September 30, 1966, the wing had lost 18 F-4Cs in the previous six months (including eight that September) and 22 aircrew. Morale was predictably low.

In an effort to improve the wing's fortunes, he and Capt J. B. Stone planned a mission for January 2, 1967 in which his F-4Cs would fake the QRC-160 pod-jamming formations, call-signs, Doppler navigation checks and speeds of the usual F-105D bombers. Rules of engagement which normally required visual identification of VPAF aircraft, denying F-4s the advantage of their beyond visual range (BVR) AIM-7s, were replaced by a free-fire zone with no other US aircraft in the way.

Although bad weather initially grounded the MiG-21s, their controllers belatedly allowed them to take off as the F-4 armada passed over their base en route to Hanoi. Col Olds then turned his fighters back towards Noi Bai and had to cancel the free-fire option as the next formation of F-4s posing as "Thuds" was due in. He then noticed the first of the MiG-21s as they popped up out of a ten-tenths cloud base, expecting to find F-105s. Their GCI was taken by surprise too, failing to order them to withdraw and regroup. Instead, individual VPAF pilots had to fend for themselves, and no fewer than seven – around half the active MiG-21 force – were shot down.

Interestingly, four of the MiG-21s were destroyed by AIM-7Es in textbook high-altitude, full-systems launches at a time when overall Sparrow missile reliability was running at about ten per cent. Col Olds' own opening attack suffered from familiar missile problems nevertheless. He fired four, and all failed to guide onto a MiG-21 because it dived back into clouds, fooling the missiles' infrared seeker heads.

Col Robin Olds (leaning on the AIM-9B's seeker head) with his 433rd TFS troops. As Olds explained to the author some years after the Vietnam War, "The relationship between the pilot and the groundcrews is something not understood or thought of by people up above. Any MiG kill credit went to the crew chief and his aircraft, not to the pilot's own assigned aircraft. Because of the arduous maintenance schedules, it wasn't always possible for a pilot to fly his own aircraft. As a matter of fact, flying your own bird was a rare occasion. Yet the system worked. Assignment of aircraft to pilots boosted morale, but is also enhanced individual and unit pride."

55

The air-to-air weapon of choice within the VPAF, the R-3S "Atoll" infrared homing missile was a direct copy of the American AIM-9B Sidewinder. The weapon was 2.8m long, with a diameter of 127mm. It weighed 75.3kg and had a blast-fragmentation warhead. The R-3S could be launched at an altitude of up to 21,000m, and had an effective range of 8000m.

His No 2 jet, flown by 1Lts Ralph Wetterhahn and Jerry Sharp, achieved a full-systems lock-on to another MiG-21, however, as the former recalled. "The AIM-7E impacted forward of the stabilizer. A fireball appeared and the MiG flew through it, continued for an instant and then swapped ends, shedding portions of the aft section."

Fortunately for the VPAF all the pilots ejected, but the beaten 921st FR withdrew from combat for three months to re-train, acquire new jets and revise tactics. Conversely, spirits at Ubon were restored. Col Olds' reputation was further enhanced too. As "Triple Nickel" MiG killer Capt Don Logeman told the author, "The Robin Olds of this world are born for combat, not the Pentagon, and I would have flown as his wingman over Hanoi in 1967 even if we had been armed with .45-cal. pistols!"

At the end of his tour Col Olds reported, "Our basic job over here is to bomb targets, not chase MiGs. However, we liked the MiGs because they kept our morale up. All fighter pilots have a love for aerial battle. It's a great feeling to launch a missile at a MiG even if that missile misses. At least you feel useful!"

Col Olds never underestimated the effectiveness of the MiG-17 either. In his report on the May 20, 1967 dogfights in which two MiG-21s and four MiG-17s were shot down from a defensive "wagon wheel" formation, he commented, "The MiG-17, when used as it was on this day, was a more formidable opponent than the MiG-21. The MiGs are growing more aggressive. The MiG-21s on January 2 (Operation *Bolo*) were not the problem that the MiG-17s were on this day."

Among the VPAF pilots who took to their KM-1 ejection seats on January 2, 1967 were future aces Vu Ngoc Dinh and Nguyen Van Coc. The latter pilot recalled:

The MiG-21s were taking off one by one, and each of the first four was shot down by Phantom IIs. The same fate was waiting for the leader of the second formation. This serious loss was due to the late take-off of the alert aircraft, indecisiveness in the Central Command Post and a faulty concept – we expected F-105s.

ENGAGING THE ENEMY

Both crewmembers in the Phantom II coordinated missile attacks. The WSO acquired the target with the radar in "search" mode, using a hand controller to direct the antenna. With a target on the screen, he locked the radar onto it. The pilot had a repeat of the display on his radar screen, with the "blip" moving downwards on a vertical line as the range closed.

At the centre of the Allowable Steering Error (ASE) circle on the screen appeared a white "pipper" or "death dot", 2 mil across (this measurement corresponding to an area two feet wide on a target at a range of 1,000 yards), and this was repeated on the combining glass screen of his lead computing optical sight system. The ASE circle increased or decreased in size depending on range, and if the target moved inside minimum missile launch range a "Break-X" symbol appeared on the screen. Small tabs on the display showed the aircraft's roll attitude, and an analogue range bar inside the ASE circle showed the rate of change in distance to the target.

When the range was correct for an AIM-7 launch, the "pipper" changed from white to green. Radar lock would break if the "pipper" drifted outside ASE limits, or if the radar was "looking" at the target below an "altitude" line in which it was seen against a background of terrain rather than sky. Radar reflections from the ground ("clutter") blanked out target returns.

In ideal conditions, the radar needed four seconds to settle as the system prepared to launch, counted down by the WSO. If the pilot had engaged the switch on his missile panel that said "Interlocks In," he could then pull the trigger and the AIM-7 would be ejected and fire up its motor when the radar had "settled." Without "Interlocks In," the launch could take place at any time, but with less chance of a hit.

The "pipper" had to be kept on target throughout the missile's flight (20 seconds for a target two miles ahead) or it would not guide. For a head-on launch, minimum range was three miles — too distant for the crew to make an accurate visual target identification.

The 1972 Field Modification 556 moved all missile switches to the throttle lever for ease of operation.

For an AIM-9 launch, the pilot put the "pipper" on target, set his missile selector switch to "heat" and got a low growl in his headset, increasing in pitch as the missile picked up a strong infrared target. It could then be launched and left to find its target.

Through the monsoon months of 1967, MiG-17s shouldered air defense duties, but the 921st FR resumed combat in late April. Its improved missile skills cost the USAF two "Wolfpack" F-4Ds that summer, including 66-0238, which was one of four 555th TFS jets downed on August 23, 1967. Its destruction gave Nguyen Van Coc his second kill. His combat report from the mission read as follows:

> The leader, Nguyen Nhat Chieu, and I went the long way round to get into a better attacking position behind the enemy formation. He fired an AAM, bringing down a Thunderchief, while I successfully attacked a Phantom II with an R-3S. In the meantime, the leader began another attack with his second missile, but it missed. He went into cloud overhead, only to reappear moments later, firing his cannon. I also attacked the Phantom II using a missile, but I was too close and I strayed into Nguyen Nhat Chieu's line of fire as he dived from above. My aeroplane was damaged by his cannon fire, but all the controls were working normally so I asked to carry on the engagement. However, command ordered me to return to base.

Apart from illustrating the VPAF's dictorial GCI procedures, this account shows the ever-present dangers of "blue on blue" attacks. Indeed, some VPAF pilots were shot down by their own SAMs and AAA. Amongst those to have a close shave were Nguyen Van Coc and his wingman Dang Ngoc Ngu (another seven-victory ace), who took off from the forward base at Tho Xuan, away from their usual GCI, in May 1968 and were greeted by AAA fire from the ill-informed local defenses. Worse was to come during this mission, as a clearly rattled Nhu almost attacked a second pair of MiG-21s, mistaking them for American fighters.

May 1967 was a month in which the USAF seemed to have re-established the kinds of kill-to-loss ratios it had achieved in Korea. Phantom IIs shot down five MiG-21s and ten MiG-17s. Seven MiG-17s were destroyed on May 13 alone during what proved to be one of the biggest aerial battles of the war. In return, only two F-4s were lost that month, both to MiG-17s, and the MiG-21's score was zero.

One of the lost Phantom II pilots, from the 366th TFW, was Col Norman Gaddis. His Phantom II was hit by Lt Ngo Duc Mai's MiG-17 on May 12, and he became the first USAF colonel to be imprisoned in the infamous "Hanoi Hilton." Using an increasingly successful MiG-17 and MiG-21 tactic, Ngo Duc Mai had noticed that Col Gaddis' jet had been damaged by AAA and was lagging behind. He was quickly despatched by several well aimed cannon rounds fired from Mai's MiG-17.

Six more MiGs were destroyed on May 20 in a battle that Col Olds described as "an exact replica of the dogfights of World War II." One 8th TFW Phantom II was set ablaze by the gunfire from an enemy fighter in an engagement that once again involved two large groups of MiG-17s, with the MiG-21s keeping a low profile. This situation continued until August 23, 1967, with the 921st FR failing to claim a confirmed kill in more than three months, despite *Rolling Thunder* reaching its climax during the summer of 1967. From then on things changed dramatically.

Up to February 28, 1968, 22 US aircraft, including five USAF F-4s, were lost in the air in exchange for 20 MiGs. Only four MiG-21s were claimed by the Phantom

II units. Overall, the 921st FR racked up a 17-to-1 kill/loss ratio in its favor during this period, although three kills by F-4Ds in February lowered the ratio to 4.5-to-1.

The MiG-21 had by now become a worrying threat to the American war effort. VPAF pilots had learned to approach the enemy formations from low altitudes, where USAF aircraft radars struggled to pick them up against "ground clutter." They would launch their missiles in the blind spots of the strike force and then escape either to China or to their own airfields, where, until October 1967, they were safe from air attack.

The 921st FR's engagement on November 8, 1967 showed just how successful the more aggressive MiG-21 tactics had become. Noi Bai received a warning at 0800 hrs that F-105s were inbound to Hanoi, but the base had already launched two jets as the first "standing patrol" mounted by the unit. Nguyen Hong Nhi and Nguyen Dang Kinh had taken off, flying low to avoid US radar and their own SAM batteries. They were thus well placed to meet the 555th TFS MiGCAP at the head of the formation.

At 17,000ft, some 25 miles from Yen Bai, pilots from both sides made visual contact with each other, and the Phantom IIs broke away to fend off the oncoming MiG-21s. Nguyen Hong Nhi quickly turned in behind the F-4D flown by Maj William Gordon and 1Lt Richard Brenneman. He fired an "Atoll" which exploded in the Phantom II's tailpipe and the aircraft's tail unit broke away. Maj Gordon ejected and was recovered, but his back-seater became a PoW.

US pilots were finding that the little air-to-air instruction they had received worked in combat. Capt Don Logeman recalled, "We were taught to engage the MiG-17 at as high an altitude as you could get him and the MiG-21 as low as you could get him in order to capitalize on their maneuvering disadvantages relative to the F-4."

Usually, MiG-21s would tackle the F-4 CAP flights while MiG-17s went for the bombers, although on December 17, 1967 they reversed roles and an 8th TFW F-4D was downed by a MiG-17 while MiG-21s destroyed a 388th TFW F-105D.

Some Phantom II pilots devised unofficial tactics for their own squadrons based on their experience as a way of bucking the Tactical Air Command (TAC) "welded wing" formation that so limited their range of action in a fight. Maj Phil Handley later

MiG-21PF 4326 with 13 red stars, one of which recorded Nguyen Van Coc's seventh claim (an F-4B Phantom II from VF-92 downed on May 7, 1968). Although the MiG-21 was considered less robust than the MiG-17, it offered its pilots limited armor-plated protection, unlike the F-4. Its simple mechanical systems were also quite sturdy, whereas one well-placed bullet could cause a rapid loss of hydraulic fluid in the Phantom II, with consequent control loss. Although cannon-armed MiG-21s had only five seconds of firing time, one 30mm shell in the wrong place could cripple an F-4. This photograph, taken at Noi Bai in May 1968, was released to the world's press, after which several western publications claimed that the 13 red stars on the nose of 4326 denoted the success of a single pilot, namely the fictitious "Colonel Tomb." In fact, these markings represented the victories of a number of 921st FR pilots up to that stage in the war.

devised what he called "fluid two" tactics. These were a variation on the US Navy's standard, widely spaced but mutually supportive four-ship formation.

Col Bob Ross modified another well-established naval tactic with his "combat weave," where the two pairs in a flight flew a series of criss-cross patterns with each other near the target in order to cover the flight's rear from a surprise attack.

MiG-21 tactics evolved too. New attack techniques included rear approaches at low altitude by a pair of fighters, which then zoom-climbed behind the F-4 escort flights at the rear of the strike and picked them off, before diving away supersonically. As previously mentioned in this chapter, on August 23, 1967, three jets from a 555th TFS "Ford" four-ship F-4D flight were destroyed in this way, with two falling to "Atolls" and one to fuel starvation – a fourth jet avoided the MiGs but was downed by AAA over the target area. Following this and other reversals, extra MiGCAP Phantom IIs were placed to each side of the strike force.

The arrival of a new batch of 29 Soviet-trained pilots in 1968 was another boost for the 921st FR. The new pilots further developed well-coordinated supersonic attack tactics that targeted vulnerable sections of the strikers, damaged or disorientated stragglers or fuel-starved fighters searching for tankers. Often, the MiG-21s would attack in a pair, with the second aircraft three miles "in trail" behind the leader. Also, with increased confidence, they began to make a second pass if the MiGCAP flights had not pursued them after their initial attacks.

Coordinated assaults were also devised using bigger groups of MiG-17s in coordinated attacks from several different directions. Once the strike force had been distracted, and possibly broken up, the MiG-21s would dive from their high "perch" and make their contribution to the mayhem. Their results improved accordingly. In October 1967 only two MiG-21s were lost against three F-4s. The following month the statistics were 6-to-2 in their favor, whereas in July of that same year the score had been 13-to-0 to the F-4 units. When President Johnson ended *Rolling Thunder* on March 31, 1968, the previous month's losses had been about equal for both sides.

MiG pilots also learned to surprise their enemy by forward-deploying flights to airfields further to the south. Nguyen Van Coc's second F-4 kill on May 7, 1968 came during a patrol by the three flights of MiG-21s that had been specially deployed to Tho Xuan, in central North Vietnam, to intercept US Navy strikes. He recalled:

Dang Ngoc Ngu noticed two F-4s some five kilometers to starboard, and due to the very cloudy weather, he had to make a right turn for the attack, but was unable to get into a firing position. I could not follow my leader, and was left behind by seven kilometers. I was looking for him, but noticed that I was running low on fuel and wanted to return to Tho Xuan. At that moment I noticed a Phantom II (F-4B) ahead of me. I went after him and launched two missiles at a distance of 1500m. The Phantom II crashed in flames into the sea, after which both of us made a safe landing at Tho Xuan.

Phantom IIs also benefited from new technology in their ongoing struggle to regain the upper hand over the resurgent VPAF. EC-121s equipped with QRC-248 could interrogate the IFF transponders in MiGs, identifying their type and exact location.

The EC-121 commander commented in the USAF's *Red Baron* war analysis, "It was somewhat frightening to realise that in the past there had been so many aircraft we hadn't seen." On October 23 and 26, 1967, coordinated efforts by these aircraft and Ubon F-4s destroyed four MiGs. During *Linebacker* this capability allowed a relaxation of the visual ID Rules of Engagement, thus improving BVR AIM-7 results.

Also, F-4C crews finally got guns when the 366th TFW fitted SUU-16/A (later SUU-23/A) gun pods to their Phantom IIs. The first gun kills occurred in May 1967 – a month in which 15 MiGs were claimed and three F-4s lost. Fitting QRC-160 ECM pods to Phantom IIs also allowed them to stay closer to the strike formation, thus giving them better SAM protection. To help compensate for the unreliability of the AIM-4 Falcon, two F-4Ds in each 8th TFW MiGCAP carried SUU-23/A gun pods, and some were unofficially re-wired for AIM-9s as "Fast CAP" Phantom IIs.

Col Olds had rejected the gun pod for his fighters, but he told Korean War ace Col "Boots" Blesse of the 366th TFW that he would be "interested to see the results". His reservations were in the interests of his own pilots, untrained as they were for close combat. "I had no intention of giving any of my young pilots the temptation to go charging off to engage MiG-17s with guns. They would have been eaten alive."

Olds had more respect for the abilities of those MiG pilots, and their managers, than he felt for some of the senior figures who were running the American war plan:

> The people in the higher echelons barely had a clue. They had very little to do with the nitty gritty of the fight. On the other side, whoever ran the MiG operations went about the task with great care early on. Opportunities for engagements were therefore extremely rare at first.

Attacks on MiG airfields in 1967 destroyed 30 VPAF fighters on the ground, in addition to the 37 (17 MiG-21s) jets destroyed by USAF Phantom IIs. In return, the USAF stated that nine F-4C/Ds were lost in aerial combat, six of them to MiG-21s.

Three MiG-killer F-4Ds in one formation. 66-7554/OY, with Maj R. D. Howerton and 1Lt T. L. Voigt at the controls, shot down a MiG-17 on February 14, 1968 while serving with the 555th TFS/8th TFW. 66-8688/PN, flown by Capt R. H. Boles and 1Lt R. B. Battista, destroyed a MiG-21 on February 6, 1968 when assigned to the 433rd TFS/8th TFW. And, finally, Lt Col C. D. Westphal and Capt J. S. Feinstein of the 13th TFS/432nd TRW used 66-7501 for their MiG-21 kill on October 13, 1972.

Aerial engagements continued occasionally in the four years between *Rolling Thunder* and the final battles. MiG-21s destroyed two F-4Ds on December 18, 1971 – their first since *Rolling Thunder* – when Snr Lts Le Than Dao and Vo Si Giap surprised the Phantom IIs as they covered a helicopter operation, shooting them down, and causing a third F-4D to run out of fuel. Giap's MiG-21 was damaged by F-4s on May 8, 1972, and he died attempting to crash-land his precious jet rather than obeying GCI orders to eject.

USAF MiG kills resumed on February 21, 1972, when Maj Robert Lodge and 1Lt Roger Locher (flying F-4D fitted with APX-81 *Combat Tree*) of the 555th TFS/432nd TRW fired three AIM-7E-2s from up to 11 miles away to destroy a MiG-21 with a "secondary explosion that appeared like a large POL explosion with a fireball." Capts Fred Olmstead and Gerald Volloy launched their AIM-7s from eight miles to kill another MiG-21 on March 30. At last the F-4's BVR capability was being regularly used.

In a major clash on April 16, 1972, an unusually large group of ten MiG-21s and twenty MiG-17s ventured over the Ho Chi Minh trail to face an American air strike. Three MiG-21s were shot down, despite US missile unreliability again plaguing the F-4 crews. Maj Dan Cherry fired all four of his AIM-9s at an in-range MiG-21 and his wingman followed his attack up with a salvo of four AIM-7s, but none of the missiles achieved a hit. Finally, Cherry pulled back into correct AIM-7 range and downed the MiG with a single missile.

On May 10, 1972, as *Linebacker II* began, some of the war's most violent air engagements took place, beginning over Noi Bai at 0830 hrs. The 432nd TRW lost one of its most valuable members on this date when Maj Robert Lodge (and his WSO Capt Roger Locher, who survived) was shot down and killed by a MiG-19 shortly after he had shot down a MiG-21 (probably flown by Cao San Khao) for his third kill.

Three MiG-21s were claimed in return by the 555th TFS, including the first for future ace Capt Steve Ritchie. Lt Nguyen Van Ngai was one of five VPAF pilots killed that day, and May as a whole was disastrous for the Vietnamese, with 11 pilot losses and US attacks which the VPAF perceived as a concerted onslaught against its assets. The air force stood down to reconsider tactics once again.

Throughout the summer of 1972, USAF and US Navy F-4 crews frequently caught MiG-21s at their most vulnerable as they took off or landed at Noi Bai or Kep. On July 8, the day that Capts Steve Ritchie and Chuck DeBellevue downed two more MiG-21s, the pilot of one of these jets had attempted to land at three different Phantom II-patrolled airfields before being downed approaching the third, Gia Lam.

And the VPAF was suffering from a lack of experienced MiG-21 crews by mid 1972. Amongst the veteran pilots no longer flying was Nguyen Van Coc, who had ceased combat operations in 1969 – he nevertheless retained his top ace status with nine kills through to war's end.

On August 28, 1972, the USAF was at last able to crown its first Vietnam aces when Capt Steve Ritchie and his WSO destroyed their fifth MiG. DeBellevue, went on to score a sixth victory the following month with Capt John Madden. The USAF's third F-4 ace was WSO Capt Jeffrey Feinstein, who got his fifth MiG kill on October 8 with Lt Col Curtis Westphal, who described the event:

> Capt Feinstein obtained a radar contact at 17 nautical miles. *Red Crown* confirmed the contact as being the bandits, and our flight closed on a front quarter attack. Due to the presence of "friendlies" in the area, we decided not to fire at that point. After closing to one mile, Capt Feinstein obtained a visual contact on one of the two MiG-21s. We turned left to engage and fired three AIM-7 missiles. All eight members of the flight observed the second AIM-7 hit the MiG-21 in the aft section, at which point it burst into flames. We saw the MiG pilot eject at approximately five seconds after missile impact.

The MiG-21 was being flown by inexperienced pilot Nguyen Van Tue, who hesitated too long when ordered to take evasive action.

Also claiming his sixth, and final, kill (an F-4E) in October 1972 was Nguen Duc Soat, who had shot down two F-4Es in June 1972, an F-4E and an F-4D (from the 405th FW, detached to Udorn) in July and a US Navy F-4J in August. Otherwise, October was a bad month for the MiG-21 units, with seven jets lost to USAF F-4s and five more in airfield raids. Forty pilots were killed (to all causes) in 1972 out of 120 on strength.

Despite these losses, tactics continued to improve as the year progressed, with pilots learning to restrict their use of IFF to defeat *Combat Tree*. However, nothing could protect their bases and supplies from the 11-day fury of *Linebacker II*, which saw B-52s and other bombers carrying out the devastating night strikes that many had advocated in 1965. Although these missions marked the climax, and finale, of the main air war, MiG-21s contributed little to the defensive effort.

Although the VPAF claimed seven F-4s shot down (against three MiG-21 casualties) during these night raids, the USAF recorded only two losses, of which F-4E 67-0234 of the 4th TFS/432nd TRW, downed on December 27/28, 1972, was the last to be destroyed by a MiG-21. It was also the only US aircraft lost in air-to-air combat at night during the entire war. That Phantom II, on a *Linebacker II* B-52 MiGCAP, and the 13th TFS F-4E (67-0292, itself a former MiG-killing aircraft) lost several hours earlier were both claimed by 921st FR pilot Tran Viet.

The final fiery moments of F-4E 69-7296 of the 366th TFW, shot down by the 921st FR's Bui Thanh Liem over Nghia Lo on June 27, 1972. The crew of the Phantom II, pilot Maj R C Miller and WSO 1Lt Richard H McDow, both successfully ejected. Miller was subsequently rescued by a USAF Search And Rescue team, but his WSO was captured before he could be extracted.

1. Intercom system controls
2. Boarding steps position indicator
3. Automatic flight control system panel
4. Drag chute control handle
5. VOR/ILS control panel
6. Fuel control panel
7. Engine control panel (outboard)
8. Throttles
9. Emergency oxygen control (on seat)
10. Canopy selector
11. Utility panel (left)
12. Oxygen control panel
13. External stores emergency release
14. Flaps, landing gear and external lights indicators and controls
15. Canopy emergency release handle
16. Landing gear control handle
17. Eight-day clock
18. True airspeed indicator
19. Missile status panel
20. Radar altimeter
21. Emergency brake control handle
22. Missile control panel
23. Range indicator
24. Airspeed and Mach indicator
25. Radar scope and sight reticule controls
26. Sight mode knob
27. Optical sight unit
28. Attitude director indicator (ADI)
29. Air refueling indicator lights
30. Standby magnetic compass
31. Angle-of-attack indexer
32. Angle-of-attack indicator
33. Accelerometer
34. Weapons delivery mode selector panel
35. Weapons station and control panel
36. CRT for azimuth/elevation (AN/APR-25/26 or APS-107A RHAW)
37. AN/ASG-22 lead-computing sight
38. Rudder pedals
39. Oil, hydraulic and pneumatic pressure gauges
40. Navigation function selector panel
41. Emergency attitude indicator
42. Vertical velocity indicator
43. Altimeter
44. Fire/overheat warnings
45. Internal fuel quantity indicator
46. Engine indicators (top to bottom, in pairs – fuel flow, tachometer, exhaust gas temperature, exhaust nozzle position indicator)
47. Sub-panel telelights
48. Arresting hook control handle
49. Trim button
50. Bomb release (missile trigger behind handgrip on control column)
51. Air refueling release button
52. Generator control panel
53. Communication (radio) control panel
54. Utility panel
55. Circuit breaker panel
56. IFF panel
57. Navigation control panel
58. Emergency harness release handle
59. Lower ejection handle

MiG-21MF COCKPIT

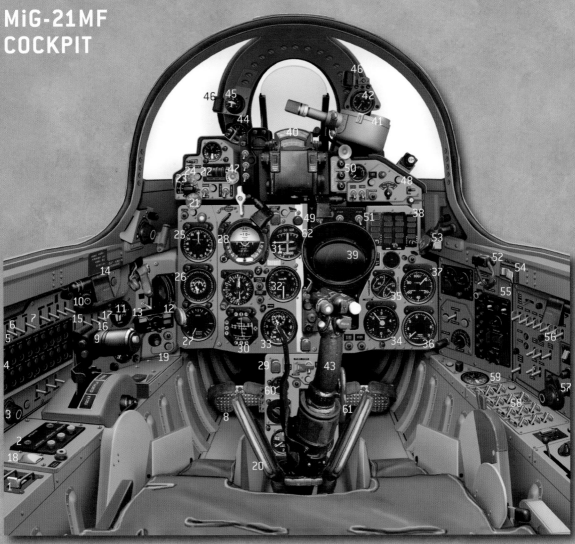

1. Oxygen controls

2. Flap controls

3. Pilot's high-altitude suit heat and ventilation.

4. Circuit breakers for Lazur-M GCI

5. Pilot's seat height adjustment

6. Engine exhaust position control

7. Cockpit temperature controls

8. Rudder pedals

9. Throttle, with controls for radio, airbrake and target range

10. Drag 'chute deployment handle

11. Oxygen flow indicator

12. Undercarriage lever

13. Flap and airbrake position indicators

14. Cockpit lamp (left)

15. Nose-cone manual/auto operation

16. Emergency afterburner "off" switch

17. Air re-start (ground start for engine to left of Lazur circuit-breakers)

18. Drag 'chute jettison control

19. Autopilot controls

20. KM-1 ejection seat operating handles (manual override is on right knee-guard, red)

21. Emergency undercarriage brakes

22. Range calculator

23. Weapon selector

24. Gun reload button

25. Air speed indicator

26. Altimeter

27. Radio altimeter

28. Artificial horizon

29. External fuel tank jettison

30. Target position indicator for GCI

31. Turn and bank indicator

32. Mach meter

33. Clock

34. Fuel gauge

35. Hydraulic pressure gauge

36. Exhaust gas temperature gauge

37. Engine RPM

38. System status lights panel

39. Radar scope

40. Target range indicator (ASP-PFD-21A optical gunsight)

41. SSh-45-1000S gun camera

42. Angle of attack indicator

43. Control column with autopilot, target tracking, trim buttons and gun firing button on rear of column

44. Airframe over-stress indicator

45. SPO-3 Sirena-3 (or later) radar warning receiver indication

46. Dangerous angle of attack warning lights

47. De-icing control

48. IFF control panel

49. Master emergency indicator light

50. Radar control panel

51. Optical aiming system control lights

52. Cockpit lamp (right)

53. Emergency landing gear control

54. Emergency canopy release

55. Control panel for radio

56. Main selector switches for missiles, radar, stores, avionics, nose-cone systems

57. IFF code selector and control light

58. No 3 engine control panel (batteries, fuel pumps, generators, transformers)

59. Pressure gauge for emergency systems

60. Weapons/stores controls

61. Emergency nose-gear lowering handle

62. White stripe for pilot to "center" the control column for spin recovery

Poor weather and heavy cloud were among the main obstacles to US air attacks on North Vietnam, particularly in the monsoon season. The LORAN (Long Range Navigation) system allowed bombing from above cloud during *Linebacker* missions, although accuracy was often poor and the F-4s were more vulnerable to SAMs and MiGs. This bomb-laden 555th TFS F-4D (66-8737) has a LORAN antenna above its fuselage.

En route to a MiGCAP orbit over North Vietnam, an F-4D and an F-4E from the 432nd TRW still carry their centerline fuel tanks. This two-ton weight (when full) had to be dropped prior to combat, and this could only be done at set speeds according to the amount of fuel remaining in the tanks. Usually, this meant a speed reduction to 375kts in straight and level flight – the last thing a pilot needed when he was heading for a MiG engagement. In many cases losing the tank caused damage to the underside of the aircraft, and several Phantom IIs were brought down in this way.

The 13th TFS crew had been involved in the search for an F-111 crew when their MiGCAP was caught by MiG-21s. Tran Viet had noticed that the F-4E had become separated from its flight during the engagement, and he was able to hit it with an "Atoll."

That night, he was sent on one of his unit's six attempted B-52 interceptions. Two other MiG-21s also sortied in an attempt to draw one of the MiGCAP Phantom II flights away from the bombers while Tran Viet, as the "trailer," approached at low altitude before making a zoom climb attack. As he began his ascent in full afterburner, he found himself behind another incoming MiGCAP flight that included the 4th TFS F-4E flown by Capt John Anderson and 1Lt Brian Ward, flying at low altitude 30 miles from Hanoi.

When he had closed to within two miles of the Phantom IIs, Tran Viet fired a pair of "Atolls" at the number four aircraft in the flight, turning it into a yellow fireball. The crew successfully ejected, although Capt Anderson broke both of his arms when he left the jet at high speed. The rest of the MiGCAP set off after Tran Viet, but he "hit the deck" and out-ran them.

The last F-4 success against MiG-21s also came at night, and it involved "Globe" flight (two 4th TFS F-4Ds) which was on a night MiGCAP protecting B-52 strikes in Route Package III on January 7, 1973. Twenty-eight-year-old Capt

Paul Howman and 1Lt Lawrence Kullman were, unusually, flying with their navigation lights on, as their wingman's radar had failed and he had to follow them visually. Capt Howman reported:

> About five minutes after arriving on station, we were advised by "*Red Crown*" that a MiG-21 was airborne out of Noi Bai and heading towards the inbound strike force. When we got to about 30 miles from the MiG's position, I called "Globe 02" to jettison the centerline fuel tank. We pulled up the nose to reach 300 kts in order to punch them off, and I hit the switch and dumped the nose to accelerate. At 16 miles "*Red Crown*" gave clearance to fire. At ten miles I got a visual on an afterburner plume. Calling the MiG out to the back-seater, I put the pipper on him.
>
> At six miles we got a good full-systems lock-on. Range was about four miles when I squeezed the trigger, with the ASE circle expanding. The missile (AIM-7E-2) came off, did a little barrel roll and detonated 50ft short of his tail. I squeezed off another one at two miles range. This one just pulled some lead and went straight for the MiG. It hit him in the fuselage and the aeroplane exploded and broke into three big, flaming pieces.

MiG pilot Capt Hoang Cong was listed as "killed in action" on that day. The F-4 crew had been fortunate to survive this encounter, as their centerline tank had in fact failed to leave the jet. Because of what the *Red Baron* report called "crew coordination problems," a circuit breaker had been pulled at the wrong time and the tank stayed on. The rear-mounted AIM-7s had made long, half-inch deep dents in it as they roared past en route to the MiG, luckily without penetrating the tank.

The use of navigation lights on night interceptions seems illogical, but it showed that MiG-21 pilots were not alone in trying to adapt daytime flying techniques to nocturnal operations. On December 28, 1972, the tenth night of the massive B-52 *Linebacker* assault, 555th TFS F-4D crew Maj Harry McKee and Capt John Dubler, operating as "Colby 01," were vectored onto a single MiG-21 that was heading for an in-bound B-52 "cell" of three bombers. Concerned at the possibility of causing an airborne collision with any of the 15 similar cells, plus their support aircraft, "Colby" flight had their lights on high-visibility "flash" mode throughout a successful AIM-7 launch which destroyed the MiG and killed its pilot, Capt Vu Xuan Thieu. After the mission, Maj McKee reported:

> I was only briefed for two kinds of tactics for night missions. If it was a non-maneuvering engagement like this one was I'd leave my lights on bright and keep "02" (wingman) on my wing. I'd have him lock on the target and fire also (both Phantom IIs hit Thieu's MiG). On the other hand, if it was a maneuvering engagement I'd send "02" home. You just can't maneuver two aeroplanes at night.

Interestingly, the VPAF account of Thieu's fate is very different, for its states that he evaded numerous missiles from the F-4 escorts before ramming a B-52 and destroying it. According to USAF records, both the B-52Ds lost that night were hit by some of the 60+ SAMs launched at their section of the attacking force.

STATISTICS AND ANALYSIS

In attempting to account for the ratios of kills versus losses for the rival fighter forces, it could be argued that the VPAF had so many potential targets that USAF losses should have been higher. In practice, the communists were forced to conserve their small force, faced with typical odds of six-to-one against them, and strike when they had the advantage. Conversely, the small numbers of MiGs encountered by F-4 pilots on most missions obviously limited their kill opportunities, although proportionately they consistently reduced the MiG-21 force throughout the war.

The overall numbers of aerial victories were affected by many factors, but mainly by the success of the VPAF's GCI controllers in Hanoi and Haiphong, the lack of appropriate air-to-air training for USAF pilots and specific failures of equipment, notably air-to-air missiles. Of the 612 AIM-7 Sparrow missiles fired during the war, only 56 registered kills – a total success rate of just nine per cent.

The simpler AIM-9 Sidewinder was twice as successful, with 81 kills from 454 launches. Early versions used in *Rolling Thunder* were unable to follow a target turning at much more than 3g, and MiG pilots soon learned how to avoid them if they saw a hostile launch. Of the 187 AIM-9s fired between 1965–68, 105 failed to guide at all and only 29 scored lethal hits.

Many F-4 pilots felt that they would have downed many more MiGs if they had been given reliable weapons, including a gun for close combat. Missile unreliability continued well into *Linebacker*, and was recognised in an official CHECO report which observed that "the low reliability of our AIM missiles in combat since January 1, 1972 has prompted much concern at all command levels. The number of missiles fired versus the number of enemy aircraft destroyed is indeed discouraging."

American aircraft flew 1,992,000 combat sorties during the war, many of them in complex strike packages where F-4 CAPs had to protect up to 100 strike and support aircraft. Fighting off MiGs was just one of their many tasks, and crews were usually obliged to stay close to their charges, rather than being drawn away to take on the MiG threat. Conversely, VPAF pilots had just one task to perform – shoot down the enemy.

Comparing kill-loss statistics remains difficult. Both sides employed rigorous checking procedures for each claim before awarding kills, but there are still many disparities. For example, the VPAF claimed to have shot down 74 USAF F-4s, but only 27 of these "victories" actually match up with US statistics, including 17 F-4Es downed in June–September 1972. The USAF accepted that it lost 50 aircraft to MiG-21s from August 23, 1967 through to December 28, 1972, of which 36 were Phantom IIs.

Confusingly, in some cases, MiG pilots made no official claim for F-4s whose crews later said that they had been hit by missiles fired by MiG-21s. Conversely, on many other occasions "Fishbed" pilots claimed F-4s that surviving USAF crews attributed to SAMs or AAA. Exact analysis of the circumstances surrounding these shoot downs is no longer possible in most cases, and doubts still persist over the claims made by both sides.

The following action serves as a typical example of the 34 disputed claims to arise from USAF F-4 clashes with VPAF MiG-21s over Vietnam. On the night of May 23, 1972, an F-4D from the 435th TFS/8th TFW was flying a "Night Owl" forward air control sortie for a strike on a POL site eight miles north of the DMZ. According to the VPAF, the jet was intercepted over Nam Dinh by a MiG-21 from the 921st FR and shot down.

The crew of the Phantom II, Capts William Byrns and William Bean, became PoWs, and later described how they, like so many of their comrades, had been hit by ever-present AAA while making a low-level attack. It is unlikely that a MiG-21 would have been operating so far south at night, and at such a low altitude. On the other hand, there is a possibility that the MiG could have been flying from a forward base and practising for a B-52 interception when the unnamed pilot was distracted by the F-4 FAC.

Three of the VPAF's top fighter pilots discuss combat in front of their armed MiG-21PFMs at Noi Bai in late 1968. Nguyen Duc Soat (left) claimed six kills, Pham Than Ngan (center) eight and Nguyen Van Coc (right) nine. All of these successes were achieved in MiG-21s.

Allowing for the poor visibility from the cockpits of both aircraft, it is conceivable that an "Atoll" strike could have been mistaken for a hit by a SAM or AAA. Most MiG pilots would not have hung around long enough to be identified or chased by the victim's wingman.

The "lone wolf" tactics of some MiG-21 flyers also complicated the claims procedure. If the single "trailer" aircraft in a flight of three "Fishbeds" made an attack on a formation that had already been disturbed by the lead element of the trio, there would have been no VPAF witnesses to his possible success.

The enormous propaganda and morale value associated with achieving a "kill" also made over-claiming a great temptation. Very often a smoking or visibly damaged aircraft seen diving for safety after being hit could have been claimed as a victory when it actually managed to limp home. The VPAF practice of awarding full kills to any and all pilots who took part in the destruction of an enemy aircraft also meant that a single kill could be credited to two or three pilots. USAF aircrew would have been awarded a half-kill in those circumstances, although a shoot-down by an F-4 crew meant a full kill for *both* crewmen.

Kill-to-loss ratios varied considerably throughout the war. In situations like *Bolo*, where Phantom II crews could take full advantage of their jet's superior performance over the MiG-21, the ratio rose to 7-to-0 in their favor. However, for *Rolling Thunder* as a whole, the ratio swung from a 13-to-1 overall figure at the start of 1967 to 5-to-1 in the MiGs' favor by year-end. Seventeen F-4C/Ds were confirmed losses to MiG-21s during 1967, although 22 MiG-21s were claimed by Phantom II crews in return.

The balance changed again between October 1967 and the end of March 1968. In that time, 16 US aircraft were lost to MiG-21s in exchange for only five VPAF jets. MiGs were responsible for over 22 per cent of all US air losses in 1968. In 1965 that figure had been just one per cent. Clearly, better tactics and newer MiG-21 variants had markedly improved the VPAF's performance against American combat aircraft, but there was little USAF response in terms of revised strategies aimed at countering the new communist tactics.

Despite the huge differences in their missions and the size of their respective forces, there were genuine areas for comparison for the pilots on both sides. For example, most MiGCAP flights were provided by a small number of USAF units, notably the

F-4 pilots were used to working at night. In fact, a whole 8th TFW squadron, the 497th TFS "Night Owls" specialized in nocturnal operations. Few MiG-21 pilots trained for night flying until *Linebacker* attacks began, however, and despite excellent GCI, their efforts were usually frustrated by American ECM. The MiG-21PFM seen here parked alongside this MiG-21MF has been painted in an unusual overall light gray finish.

Early F-4Es with short gun barrels made their first appearance at Korat RTAFB on November 17, 1968, when 16 JV-coded aircraft flew in to replace the F-105s of the 469th TFS/388th TFW as part of Operation *47 Buck 9*. Arriving in-theater shortly after the end of *Rolling Thunder*, the unit had to wait until June 1972 to score its first MiG kill. The sharksmouths seen on these jets were a constant source of friction between the unit and higher authority, and they often vanished just prior to base inspections taking place, only to reappear soon afterwards!

555th TFS and parts of the 366th and 388th TFWs, although other units contributed for short periods. The MiG-21 effort also originated from two (originally one) units, although in smaller numbers.

"Second tourist" F-4 crews were comparatively rare, so that meant that most MiG engagements were fought by F-4 crews on short-term tours of 100 missions. The main USAF MiG killers achieved their successes over a period of a few months (two in the case of Capt John Madden, four for Capt Steve Ritchie and five each for Col Robin Olds and Capt Chuck DeBellvue). Although many MiG-21 pilots did serve in the VPAF throughout the entire war, only two of the sixteen official aces (Nguyen Hong Nhi and Dang Ngoc Ngu) flew for the full seven years of MiG-21 operations from 1966 through to the end of 1972. Of the rest, four flew for two years and four for only one – not so different from the Americans.

Leading USAF F-4 Phantom II "MiG Killers"				
Name	**Unit**	**Total Kills**	**MiG-21(s)**	**F-4 type**
Capt Charles B. DeBellevue	555th TFS/432nd TRW	6	4	F-4D/E
Capt Richard S. Ritchie	555th TFS/432nd TRW	5	5	F-4D/E
Capt Jeffrey S. Feinstein	13th TFS/432nd TRW	5	5	F-4D/E
Col Robin Olds	433rd TFS/8th TFW	4	2	F-4C
Capt Roger C. Locher	555th TFS/432nd TRW	3	3	F-4D
Maj Robert A. Lodge	555th TFS/432nd TRW	3	3	F-4D
Capt John A. Madden	555th TFS/432nd TRW	3	1	F-4D
1Lt George H. McKinney	435th TFS/8th TFW	3	0	F-4D
Lt Col Robert F. Titus	389th TFS/366th TFW	3	3	F-4C
1Lt Milan Zimer	389th TFS/366th TFW	3	3	F-4C

Leading VPAF MiG-21 "Phantom II Killers"

Name	Unit	Service	Kills	Status (2005)
Nguyen Van Coc	921st FR	1967–69	9	Retired
Pham Thanh Ngan	921st FR	1967–69	8	
Nguyen Hong Nhi	921st/927th FR	1966–72	8	Director-General of Vietnam Civil Aviation
Mai Van Cuong	921st FR	1966–68	8	Deputy Air Force Commander
Dang Ngoc Ngu	921st FR	1966–72	7	
Nguyen Nhat Chieu	921st FR	1965–67	6 (MiG-17 and MiG-21)	Retired
Vu Ngoc Dinh	921st FR	1966–70	6	Director of Vietnam Air Services
Nguyen Ngoc Do	921st FR	1967–68	6	
Le Thanh Dao	927th FR	1971–72	6	Political role
Nguyen Dang Kinh	921st FR	1967–68	6	
Nguyen Duc Soat	921st/927th FR	1969–72	6	Commander of Vietnamese Air Force
Nguyen Tien Sam	921st/927th FR	1968–72	6	Director General of Civil Aviation
Nguyen Van Nghia	927th FR	1972	5	Director of Civil Aviation Training

Photographed on October 11, 1972 – the day before the 35th FS returned to Kunsan, in South Korea, from Korat RTAFB – this scoreboard records the squadron's six air-to-air and eight air-to-ground kills. Two other aerial victories remained unconfirmed. Maj Ernie Leuders' six "ground" kills were achieved in multiple cluster bomb unit passes on MiG bases, during which his F-4 was targeted by heavy AAA throughout. Lt Col "Fergie" Ferguson (named on the canopy rail) led a flight made up entirely of MiG killer crews when the squadron returned to Kunsan.

AFTERMATH

One of the most enduring lessons of the air war in Vietnam was the realization that success depended on effective, well coordinated command and control of air operations. It had worked for the RAF during the Battle of Britain, and it was responsible for much of the success enjoyed by the MiG-21s in Vietnam. When the MiG-21 fought without this support in subsequent conflicts it achieved no where near as many aerial victories.

The USAF's attempt to provide an integrated MiG-warning intelligence center was code-named *Teaball*. It was described by Seventh Air Force commander Gen John Vogt Jnr as "by far the most effective instrument in the battle with the MiGs." Although it did pass on to Phantom II pilots some very sophisticated information, including monitored messages from the VPAF's GCI controllers to MiG pilots, it still tended to conflict with other intelligence sources such as *Red Crown* and *Disco*, confusing the pilots. A single control center was needed, and this was in place the next time USAF Phantom IIs went to war.

When the USAF conducted its one-night blitzkreig at the very start of Operation *Desert Storm* in January 1991, its priority target was the vast, and sophisticated, Iraqi command and control network. Those attacks were carried out quickly and devastatingly, largely because of the Coalition's own highly developed command and control systems.

The USAF's TAC finally noted in the early 1970s that it had failed to provide its aircrew with the dissimilar air combat training (DACT) that might have better prepared its fighter pilots to face the small, highly maneuverable, hard-to-see MiG-17s and MiG-21s. Its initial response was the Fighter Weapons School's *Top Off* program of extra DACT sorties for F-4 pilots going to Vietnam, and a few of the crews who participated in *Linebacker II* had that experience.

In 2008, the VPAF still flies MiG-21s. This MiG-21bis displays the same style of red "bort" number and gold star "Sao Vang" insignia that the type wore 40 years previously. The only real difference is the jet's location. This MiG-21 is seen commencing its take-off run along the main runway at the former Phantom II base at Da Nang, in what was once known as South Vietnam.

Longer-term, it heeded the advice of its own *Red Baron* recommendations for "intensified ACM for all tactical fighter pilots who can reasonably expect to be involved in air-to-air combat in any future conflict." The result of that was *Red Flag*, a training scenario that some pilots consider to be more realistic than war itself.

Post-war, the Phantom II remained the USAF's premier fighter-bomber well into the 1980s, with specialist SAM-hunting "Wild Weasel" F-4Gs (converted from F-4Es) surviving in frontline service long enough to see combat in *Desert Storm*. These aircraft, flown by the 35th TFW(P), were in the vanguard of the attacks on Iraq's air defenses. RF-4Cs also flew vital "Scud" missile search sorties. However, as the Phantom II's 35th anniversary approached, it continued its steady phase-out, replaced from the late 1970s onwards by the F-16 and F-15A/C/E.

These new fighters embodied the lessons of Vietnam, and were appropriate for the wars they would fight. Making good deficiencies in the F-4, they were air-to-air fighters with excellent pilot visibility, outstanding maneuverability, excess power (enabling acceleration in a climb) from smokeless engines, a gun, much improved versions of the AIM-7 and AIM-9 and a pilot-friendly cockpit supported by digital technology. The F-15 Eagle, conceived in the late 1960s, shot down 37 Iraqi aircraft during *Desert Storm*, including advanced MiG-25s and MiG-29s, without loss. In worldwide service, Eagles have achieved an unprecedented 100-to-0 kill-to-loss ratio in combat.

Post-Vietnam, the USAF's Phantom II fleet received the slatted wings, cockpit updates and smokeless engines developed for the *Rivet Haste* F-4Es, but further development was limited by its imminent replacement. Many F-4s were exported, and in 2008 some still serve out their twilight years with a handful of air forces across the globe. Various upgrade proposals were developed, but the most extensive was the Israeli "Kurnass 2000" project, which provided a modern digital cockpit, new avionics and better engines. Phantom IIs re-entered combat several times with the Iranian and Israeli air forces, where they again tangled with MiG-21s.

For the VPAF, there was little time for celebration in 1973. As well as rebuilding its shattered facilities, the air force continued to support North Vietnamese troops in their fight with forces in the south. The VPAF anticipated some opposition from the American-trained and well-equipped South Vietnamese Air Force as communist troops prepared to move south and remove the Saigon regime in 1974–75. In practice, the invasion routed the South Vietnamese defenses, and the VPAF absorbed around 65 Northrop F-5A/E fighters (a match for the MiG-21), among many other former South Vietnamese aircraft. These jets operated alongside the MiGs until the supply of captured spare parts eventually ran out in the early 1980s.

The MiG-21 continues to serve as the principal fighter in the VPAF, with some 150 MiG-21bis fighter and MiG-21UM trainer variants still in service in 2008. They fly with five fighter regiments, including the wartime 927th FR "Lam Son," from wartime VPAF bases like Kep, but also from ex-US facilities further south such as Cam Ranh Bay. In 1996 an attempt to modernize the fighter force through the purchase of French Mirage 2000s was frustrated by a US arms export embargo. A small number of Sukhoi Su-27s serve alongside the MiG-21bis, however.

Like the Phantom II, the MiG-21 has been the subject of several modernization projects. Again, Israeli aircraft firms have been in the lead with the MiG-21-2000, providing a modern digital cockpit and a greater range of weapons. Other American and European companies also offer avionics upgrades, since many of the 56 air arms that originally received MiG-21s intend to continue operating them.

Several VPAF MiG-21 aces remained in the VPAF for many years after the war had ended, including Nguyen Van Coc, who rose to the position of commander of the air force in 2003. Fellow ace Nguyen Duc Soat, when Deputy Chief of Staff of the Vietnamese Peoples' Army, met Lt Gen Dan Leaf, Deputy Commander of US Pacific Command, in June 2007. They discussed "areas for future military cooperation." A few months later Duc Soat was presented with a medal by Russian Deputy Minister of Defense Mikhail Dmitriev for "contributions to the friendship shared between the two armies" and "strengthening the alliance" with Russia. As these high level meetings reveal, Vietnam in the 21st century has to perform a unenviable political balancing act on the world stage.

Finally, former MiG-21 pilot Pham Thuan, who claimed a B-52 destroyed in 1972, became Vietnam's first Soyuz cosmonaut in July 1980.

Many former Phantom II crew members also rose to high rank in the USAF (Steve Ritchie went one step further and ran for Congress), and their influence seems to have instilled a "fighter mentality" into Pentagon thinking in the postwar years.

FURTHER READING

Anderegg, C. R., *Sierra Hotel* (Government Reprints Press, 2001)

Belyakov, R. A. and Marmain, J., *MiG – 50 Years of Secret Aircraft Design* (Naval Institute Press, 1994)

Berger, C. (Ed.), *The US Air Force in South East Asia 1961-73* (Office of Air Force History, 1977)

Blesse, Maj Gen F. C., *"Check Six" – A Fighter Pilot Looks Back* (Champlin Fighter Museum Press, 1987)

Boniface, R., *Fighter Pilots of North Vietnam* (Authors Online, 2005)

Boyne, W. J., *Phantom in Combat* (Jane's Publishing, 1985)

Bugos, Glenn E., *Engineering the F-4 Phantom II* (Naval Institute Press, 1996)

Clodfelter, M., *The Limits of Air Power* (Free Press, 1989)

Cook, J. N., *Once A Fighter Pilot* (McGraw Hill, 1996)

Davies, Peter E., Osprey Combat Aircraft 45 – *USAF F-4 Phantom II MiG Killers 1965-68* (Osprey, 2004)

Davies, Peter E., Osprey Combat Aircraft 55 – *USAF F-4 Phantom II MiG Killers 1972-73* (Osprey, 2005)

Dorr, R F., *Air War Hanoi* (Blandford Press, 1988)

Drendel, Lou, *. . . And Kill MiGs* (Squadron Signal, 1997)

Ethell, J and Price, A., *One Day in a Long War* (Greenhill Books, 1989)

Flintham, Victor, *Air Wars and Aircraft* (Arms and Armour Press, 1989)

Francillon, Rene J., *McDonnell F-4D* (Aerofax, 1987)

Gordon, Yefim, *Mikoyan MiG-21 – Famous Russian Aircraft* (Midland, 2008)

Gordon, Yefim and Davison, P., *MiG-21 Fishbed* (Speciality Press, 2006)

Gunston, Bill, *Mikoyan MiG-21* (Osprey, 1986)

Handley, Col P., *Nickel on the Grass* (iUniverse, 2006)

Hannah, Craig C., *Striving for Air Superiority* (Texas A&M University Press, 1996)

Hanek, W (Ed.), *Aces and Aerial Victories* (Albert Simpson Historical Research Centre, 1976)

Hobson, Chris, *Vietnam Air Losses* (Midland Publishing, 2001)

Johnson, Val Ross, *Night Owl Fighter Pilot* (iUniverse, 2006)

Koran, F. et. al., *MiG-21MF/UM in Detail* (Wings and Wheels Publishing, 2004)

Logan, Don, *The 388th Tactical Fighter Wing* (Schiffer, 1995)

McCarthy, D. J. Jnr, *USAF F-4 and F-105 MiG Killers* (Schiffer, 2005)

McCarthy, Mike, *Phantom Reflections* (Praeger Security International, 2007)

McDonnell Aircraft, *NATOPS F-4 Flight Manual* (US Naval Systems Command)

McGovern, Tim, *McDonnell F-4E Phantom* (Aerofax, 1987)

Michel, M. L., *Clashes – Air Combat over North Vietnam* (Naval Institute Press, 1997)

Michel, M. L., *The 11 days of Christmas* (Encounter, 2002)

Peake, W. R., *F-4 Phantom II Production and Operational Data* (Midland, 2004)

Rasimus, Ed., *Palace Cobra – A Fighter Pilot in the Vietnam War* (St Martins Press, 2006)

Ross, Col Bob, *The Warriors* (Yucca Tree Press, 2002)

Schlight, J., *A War Too Long – the USAF in South-east Asia 1961-75* (Air Force History and Museums Program, 1996)

Schlight, J., *The Years of the Offensive 1965-68* (Office of Air Force History, 1997)

Scutts, J., *Wolfpack – Hunting MiGs Over Vietnam* (Airlife, 1987)

Skulski, P., *MiG-21bis 'Fishbed L/N'* (Ace Publications, 2000)

Spick, M., *Jet Fighter Performance, Korea to Vietnam* (Ian Allan, 1986)

Stepfer, H-H, *Walk Around MiG-21, Parts 1 and 2* (Squadron Signal 2004 & 2005)

Thompson, W., *To Hanoi and Back* (University Press of the Pacific, 2000)

Thornborough A. M., Davies P. E., *The Phantom Story* (Arms & Armour, 2000)

Toperczer, István, *Air War Over North Vietnam* (Squadron Signal, 1998)

Toperczer, István, Osprey Combat Aircraft 29 – *MiG-21 Units of the Vietnam War* (Osprey, 2001)

Van Staaveren, J., *Gradual Failure – The Air War Over North Vietnam 1965-66* (Air Force History and Museum Program, 2002)

INDEX

References to illustrations are shown in **bold**.